Dear Leslie,

May God b'

you with fresh-

see His hand on you

Jrs Carrig

12/2/17

Fresh Eyes

SEEING GOD IN THE UNEXPECTED

IRIS CARIGNAN

WESTBOW
PRESS®
A DIVISION OF THOMAS NELSON
& ZONDERVAN

This book is a work of non-fiction. Unless otherwise noted, the author
and the publisher make no explicit guarantees as to the accuracy of
the information contained in this book and in some cases, names of
people and places have been altered to protect their privacy.

WestBow Press books may be ordered through booksellers or by contacting:

WestBow Press
A Division of Thomas Nelson & Zondervan
1663 Liberty Drive
Bloomington, IN 47403
www.westbowpress.com
1 (866) 928-1240

Because of the dynamic nature of the Internet, any web addresses or links contained
in this book may have changed since publication and may no longer be valid. The views
expressed in this work are solely those of the author and do not necessarily reflect the
views of the publisher, and the publisher hereby disclaims any responsibility for them.

ISBN: 978-1-5127-5891-7 (sc)
ISBN: 978-1-5127-5892-4 (hc)
ISBN: 978-1-5127-5890-0 (e)

Library of Congress Control Number: 2016916387

Print information available on the last page.

WestBow Press rev. date: 09/21/2017

Praise for Fresh Eyes

"Fresh Eyes provides a unique glimpse into the life journey of one of God's precious children. Iris Carignan communicates through well-told stories and beautiful poetry how God engages us in the details of every day life. This collection of stories and poems allows each of us to see God through Iris' eyes. But, that is not her sole aim. Ultimately, she encourages us to see our lives and our God through fresh eyes too —eyes of faith!"

— Shawn Thornton,
pastor and best selling author

"A real privilege to read. Sparkling, funny, spiritual, caring, tender and wise. The book really held my attention by showing God interacting and intervening in normal life."

— Joel Kilpatrick,
award winning author and journalist

I dedicate this book to my best friend and husband, Larry, who continues to support, love and encourage me in all my endeavors. I also dedicate it to my mother, who, in life and death, brought blessings and miracles.

Contents

Foreword
by Joni Eareckson Tada

Before You Begin...

Every author who sits in front of a blank computer asks himself one question before he starts. And every artist who stands before a blank canvas offers up one pressing prayer: *Lord, if I'm to create something new, I need a fresh touch from you. I need to see things with fresh eyes.*

To be creative and original requires freshness. After all, untold thousands of books have already been written on the topic you want to tackle, and museums are filled with paintings of subjects that are all too familiar. The author has to ask himself, *what new slant on things can I offer?* And as he picks up his brush and palette, the artist wonders the same.

So the title of this book, *Fresh Eyes,* does not surprise me, coming from its author-artist, Iris Carignan. A gifted and skilled communicator, whether with paints or with words, my friend Iris delights in looking for a fresh perspective – not only on a canvas or computer, but on life.

And Iris knows how to *keep* a fresh point of view. Here's her secret: She looks for God in the ordinary. She watches for the Lord's touch in everyday conversations. She searches for the divine in daily living. So it doesn't surprise me that God keeps revealing himself to her in fresh new ways. She's a spiritual woman, and she sees life from the Ephesians 1:18 perspective; that is, the eyes of her heart have been enlightened.

The book you hold in your hand is a collection of everyday stories with a fresh slant. Fresh because Iris Carignan reveals the hand of God in each one. These are her stories, so they are deeply personal. But I pray they will become part of *your* story, helping the eyes of *your* heart see the fingerprints of Christ in ordinary circumstances. It's a wonderful way to live! So get started, turn the page, and be blessed by Iris' reflections. May each chapter open your eyes to the touch of God in everything you do.

Joni Eareckson Tada
Joni and Friends International Disability Center
Agoura Hills, California

Introduction

God is always present, but do we consistently see Him? Do we quickly recognize His providential hand in our lives and feel His comfort, protection and peace? As an artist, I've noticed that creative people have an innate ability to see, hear and feel what others miss. Our eyes catch the simple beauty of sunshine flickering on the leaves of a tree, or the awe of a vast horizon complimented by roses in the foreground. For some, the ears of our heart hear rhythms, rhymes and songs that partner with orchestrated poetic themes. For dancers, the quiet grace and beauty of a ballet or the rhythmic step of a masterful tango can emit passion when they harness the emotions within it. As an artist and a believer, I believe we all have an abundant capacity for seeing our great and Almighty Creator when we learn to truly look for Him.

I am blessed to see a new art student awaken to the world around them with fresh eyes. I had a student several years ago who had lost vision in one eye because of an accident. Although he had no depth perception, with help, his artistic eye developed. He then noticed things he hadn't noticed before. During class one day, he said he was now "seeing better than ever." Of course, he meant he was seeing artistically. So, as believers, why is it sometimes hard to see God working in our lives, and why are we surprised when we do? Perhaps the worries and concerns of this world blind our eyes to His mighty and miraculous ways.

Psalm 119:18 says: "Open my eyes that I may see wonderful things..." When we let God's Holy Spirit open our eyes, we can see as never before. We discover things that may have been right before our eyes, yet never noticed them. Scripture suddenly makes sense and understanding in our heart brings satisfaction. We are able to do the work of God so that He is "displayed in our lives." Spiritual eyesight doesn't happen because we intellectually decide to see better, any more than being artistic happens because we decide to become a creative type. We need the master artist and His Holy Spirit to help us.

Some of Jesus' most acclaimed miracles were His healings of the blind. One of those healings was particularly amazing because the man had been born blind. Jesus' disciples asked if he was born that way because of his own sin or the sin of his parents. Jesus said it was neither, but it was "so that the work of God might be displayed in his life" (John 9:3). The religious officials of that day couldn't figure out how Jesus did such an amazing miracle. They questioned the man, asking the same questions over and over. No matter how obvious the miracle, or how firmly he answered, they were too blind to see it. Finally he said: "One thing I do know, I was blind, but now I see."

All of the stories, songs and poems included in this collection are the result of God's unexpected intervention and interaction in my life and the lives of my friends and family. I doubt that I've had an unusual number of encounters with God, but I believe He has graciously allowed me to develop a keen spiritual focus that helps me recognize them. It is my hope that these experiences will bless, encourage and inspire you. May this collection create readiness for God's Holy Spirit to equip and develop your spiritual eyesight so you won't miss God's hand in the unforeseen circumstances of life.

If you have never experienced spiritual awakening, may these testimonies lead you to the one who can heal you of spiritual blindness—Jesus. When Jesus heals us of blindness caused by sin, God's Holy Spirit enters in so we can see as never before. Our spirit begins to dance with a partner who wrote the music of life. We have new eyes—fresh eyes.

A Psalm Inspiration

I look to the hills and the heavens.
My gaze is transfixed on the creator.
He lifts my eyes upward to Him
And draws my heart to His theater,
Of works and wonders acted out,
By nature's many thespians
With music scored about,
On sandy hills and in deep craters.

I do not slip, He does not slumber,
And so I walk protected.
He shades me with His mighty tree,
Not sun or moon, my walk affected.

My shield He is,
My shield He is,
My Lord and my perfecter.

Iris Carignan, 2014

Chapter 1

Seeing God's Protection

Surprising Vision

"Thanks for coming," I said with cheerful appreciation as the two visitors exited. It was my turn to oversee the community art museum, and though I felt privileged to display my own artwork there, the long intervals between visitors made for a boring three-hour shift. Thankfully, there had been several visitors during that day and another entered as they left. But why did I suddenly feel so fearful the minute this particular young man came in? I greeted him pleasantly and he immediately attempted a conversation with me. Feeling wary, I abandoned my usual extroverted personality. Despite his continued verbal perseverance, I remained at the front desk rather than lead him through the exhibit in my docent role. *This is silly,* I told myself. *He looks neat and clean and is very polite—why do I feel afraid?* My insides, however, began shaking, and I took further inventory of this stranger. I noticed his backpack and pondered a comment he'd made about many people being homeless after the earthquake. I tried to do some reading, but couldn't concentrate, as the fear grew even stronger. *Lord,* I prayed silently, *calm and protect me.*

Quiet reassurance whispered back with an instant recollection of a recent, yet puzzling flashback experience.

We've all heard about people having their lives flash before them during extreme moments of danger. Well, I wouldn't call tying my shoes even close to extreme danger. However, it was during this mundane morning ritual about two weeks prior to the gallery sitting, when an amazing visual flashback happened to me. Now, it wasn't a complete picture of my whole life, but it was like a mental video playing numerous times when my life had been in grave danger. I remembered how I sat stunned at this visual playback, wondering what it meant. Was I about to be in some terrible accident or some other kind of danger? I figured if that was the meaning, whatever it was would happen that day or the next. But it had been about two weeks and nothing transpired. Now, here I was feeling a sense of danger for some yet unknown reason.

I recalled my flashback. It had been a collection of unpleasant memories that had never come together in my mind. I thought it was God's way of showing me how He had protected me all my life. It started with the time I fell out of a moving car at the age of three. I vividly saw every detail of the event, including the fact that I didn't have a seatbelt on (which were not standard in autos back then). My mother had taken me to the grocery store and on the way back I got into the front seat, shut the car door and locked it. The door wasn't shut tight, and as we made a turn in the road, it flew open and I fell out. My mother quickly grabbed the edge of my skirt and stopped as safely as possible. I can still remember the roughness of the street scraping against my cheeks for what felt like several minutes. My mother told me years later that when she got out of the car and saw me laying there, my head was just inches from the rear wheel.

The next life-threatening memory was of a trip back East in a homemade camper. The open windows of it may have kept my younger brother and I cool enough, but they also sucked carbon monoxide poison from the exhaust right into the camper shell. I can still clearly remember my last thoughts and actions before losing consciousness. When I awoke, we were at our destination and this nine-year-old was sick as a dog for a week. I hadn't known until about forty-five years later what had made me so sick. After that came the vision of nearly breaking my neck on a trampoline at the age of eleven.

Just as another event came to mind, the young man in the museum startled me back into the present with some more chitchat about looking for work. Again, I did not let him pull me into conversation; I just mumbled a vague, "uh huh."

The memories continued to play across my mind as I thought about another dangerous and unusual incident. I was seventeen and visiting relatives at my grandparents' lakeside cabin in Georgia. My brothers, cousins, and I were enjoying ourselves on the lake in two rowboats when we heard the usual deafening sound of a jet taking off. At that time there was a small air force base on an island nearby and the noise was an extreme disturbance to the peacefulness of this quiet retreat. Then a very loud explosion shattered the serenity further, and we saw pieces of metal flying through the air, embedding into trees and slicing into the water just a few feet from our boats. We quickly rowed under a large tree in hopes of shielding ourselves from the debris only to have jet fuel begin to pour down on us. Rowing out from there, we made our way safely back to shore and used the nearest phone to inquire about the condition of the pilot.

There were several more incidents brought to remembrance during that vision, but the last one seemed to hold the key to why the Lord had given me this forewarning. It was the disturbing memory of a young man who had attacked me by sneaking up behind me and hitting me over the head with a rock. It had started as a beautiful afternoon and I had driven my car to a nearby field to do some sketching. I was only eighteen at the time and God had protected me in many ways that day. Thankfully, I had not been seriously molested or injured by this troubled teenager. It had even been a blessing that he stole my car, because it took him away from me. "He is a shield to those whose walk is blameless, for he guards the course of the just and protects the way of his faithful ones" (Proverbs 2:7 NLT).

I snapped back into focus on my current predicament with a fuller realization of my Lord's protection in times of danger. Yet, my insides felt like a 7.0 on the Richter scale and my anxiety did not stop. I prayed again. A very clear thought came to mind: *If the guy in the museum is there with evil intent on his mind, he will try to lure you to the back of the room.* Less than minute later, he came over to me and said that I needed to go to the back to see a painting that was "damaged." There it was! What should I do? I decided to go, but with freshened visionary wisdom, I made sure he stayed in front of me and did not let him have even one second of positional advantage over me. Pointing down at a large painting at the very back of the room and behind two large exhibit panels, he said, "See, there it is!"

I couldn't see any evidence of damage and he obviously wanted me to bend over and look closer, but I didn't. Instead, I glanced quickly at it, said "Yeah," and walked briskly back to my safety zone by the front door. Just a few minutes later, he left the museum.

About one week later, a newspaper article reported a rape in that very area and the description of the man sounded all too familiar. God had protected me again and had brought to my mind terrible events that helped me have special caution, assurance and wisdom in handling a dangerous situation. He truly is my shield and my protector.

Not many experience this kind of visionary premonition of God's protective hand. It may even seem that I have had an unusual number of rare predicaments, some of which I did not mention. That may be, but I believe that all of us would be surprised to see how many times the Lord has protected us from danger. The Word says, "Your adversary the devil walks about seeking whom he will devour" (1 Peter 5:8). We all need to be "sober and vigilant," not only in our spiritual walk, but in our daily activities. We live in a fallen world and we never know when or where the evil one may attempt to sabotage our journey. There are many times when the good Lord does allow terrible things to happen to His children, and we know that when we continue in faith, He can work all things "together for good" (Romans 8:28).

As you read through many other times of protection in my life and in the lives of friends and family, it is my prayer that they will be confirming of God's ever present hand in your own journey. The Lord may choose to reveal His merciful protection in life; but if He doesn't, we know that we should "not fix our eyes on what is seen, but what is unseen. For what is seen is temporary, but what is unseen is eternal" (2 Corinthians 4:18).

His Timely Protection

Several years ago, we met some warm and engaging people who, over time, became great friends. Sandy and Greg had just moved to our area and quickly became involved in our church and the home group we led. We seemed to have a lot in common, and our relationship clicked right away. A Cheesecake Factory had recently opened near us and we invited them to join us. Arriving at the restaurant, we found the foyer packed with waiting diners and nowhere left to sit. Sandy suggested we go into the bar area and order some appetizers and beverages while we waited for our table. "Yes! Let's."

As we sat sipping on sodas and getting better acquainted, Sandy began to share a recent story from a fellow nurse with whom she worked. A bullet had nicked her friend during a drive-by shooting. Just as she finished the story, an enormous, crashing *boom* shattered our evening. Everyone ducked. Our first thought was, *it's a drive-by shooting!* Glass was flying everywhere as chairs and tables crashed to the floor and people scattered in panic. Then we saw the source of the explosive disturbance—it was a car! It had crashed right through the front door of the restaurant and stopped just a few feet away from our table. Its rear wheels were still spinning and an elderly lady sat stunned at the wheel of the car.

There were a few people stuck under the car and several strong volunteers, including my husband, quickly teamed up to lift the heavy car off the victims. I started towards the calamity, intending to help in some way, and noticed my coat was on the floor. As I bent down to retrieve it, I suddenly felt someone grab my arm.

"That's my wife's coat," the man yelled at me. "No," I said with conflicted attention. "It's mine!" He kept insisting that it was his wife's coat, so I let him have it. By then, the people who had been run over were able to crawl out from under the car. We could see that one lady was badly injured.

It didn't take long to assess what had happened. Apparently, the driver had hit the gas pedal while the car was in reverse. It had crashed right through two tall wrought-iron and glass decorated doors, pushing them all the way into the front registration desk. Thankfully, two large parties had been seated just minutes before the accident, otherwise it would have been even worse. The reality of our timely move into the bar area and out of the danger zone quickly sank in. If we had not gone into the other area as suggested by Sandy, we would have been run over as well. The restaurant asked everyone to leave as quickly as possible and by then, the man with my coat returned it humbly, admitting it wasn't his wife's.

Still shaking inside, the four of us left and went to another restaurant. Amazingly, we were still hungry. Needless to say, our table conversation that night was filled with nervous excitement over our harrowing experience. I began telling our new friends about some of the many close calls I'd experienced since childhood, and how I'd had a vision in my closet, showing all of them. When I got to the story of the jet plane dropping a fuel tank from the sky, Sandy joked, saying she had reservations about being around me.

My response was to remind her that in each case, the Lord had been watching over me and I hadn't been gravely hurt. "So, maybe the key is to just stay close by," I quipped.

God had surely protected us that day. We had moved from the affected area only a few minutes before the crash and the car had stopped just a few feet away from us. Our friendship with Sandy and Greg continued to grow, and seeing God's hand of protection on us that evening had a lasting impact on our faith and friendship. We may have passed "through the valley of the shadow of death" (Psalm 23:4) that day, but God was there guarding us. "For He will command His angels concerning you to guard you in all your ways" (Psalm 91:11 NIV).

His Surprising Mercies

While walking our little dog one beautiful winter day, I stopped to chat with a neighbor who was returning home and about to drive up her steep driveway. She stopped, reversed her car, and set the brakes so she could retrieve the newspaper. Although we rarely had the opportunity to visit, it had been a rough week for her and the accurate timing of being at her driveway at that moment seemed to be ordained.

Our nation had experienced a horrible shooting of several children at an elementary school that same week, and my neighbor, who has two small children, was feeling the burden of this tragedy. Added to that was an extra dose of sadness with the recent loss of her dog, so I was glad to be a shoulder of comfort at that moment. After talking for about fifteen minutes, we said our goodbyes and I resumed walking my dog.

"Are you going to walk behind my car," she asked as she stopped me on the spot. "You should probably wait" she said, "as sometimes the car rolls down a bit before going up this steep driveway."

I already thought about being cautious while walking behind the vehicle, but hadn't thought it a danger since she was well aware of my presence. However, I decided to heed her warning and wait for her car to go up the hill first. It was a good thing I did, as it turned out her large SUV was still in reverse and when she hit the gas to go up, the car went careening down into the street. If I had walked behind her car, both my dog and I would have suffered severe injury and possibly death.

I stood there in awe of my Lord's protection. He had clearly spoken through my neighbor, who is a believer as well. Proverbs 2:7–8 (NLT) speaks to this when it says: "He guards the paths of the just and protects those who are faithful to him."

We never know when or where peril may lie, but we can trust that our God has plans for us and will guard our steps to help us complete them.

Heavenly Travel Insurance

My husband and I travel to Colorado on business a couple of times a year. Just before one particular trip, I had done my usual pre-arranging of things, including the care of our little Maltipoo dog, Caesar. Except for the occasional times he spent at the homes of our neighbors or family, most of the time he would go to my friend Stacy's while we were out of town. However, Stacy had a new dog that was not friendly to other dogs. As a result, I was forced to hire a nice lady who had watched him once before. Dogs don't forget, and Caesar fondly remembered Mary when she arrived. We noticed that he did not display his usual nervousness as we packed the night before our departure. He seemed to sense that Mary was going to be there with him in his own home, and that was okay with him.

The day we returned home, Mary and Caesar greeted us excitedly—Caesar with his usual jumping and dancing around, and Mary with stories of a problem while we were away. We quickly learned there had been a bad gas leak while we were out of town. It seems the brand new washer and dryer we bought just a couple of weeks before the trip had not been properly installed. Mary had called the gas company on two occasions during our short week away to report a strong smell of natural gas. The first responder from the gas company had not handled the problem well, even leaving without turning off the gas. Thankfully, the second person found the problem and fixed it.

Wow! If we had left our dog at someone else's house, as we usually did, we may not have had a house to come home to. We are so humbled and thankful to our gracious and merciful Lord who watches over our every need. As it turns out, He had done a lot of arranging for our trip too. Our Lord is the best homeowner's insurance we could ever hope for. He is our "rock... and...fortress," in whom we "take refuge" (Psalm 18:2).

Barely Safe

If you've read the preceding stories of God's protection, then what you read next may seem to put a chink in my armor or look like a slip of God's hand. You'll see how a vacation experience had me second guessing His protective hand and unearthed some lingering fears that I thought my Lord and I had firmly dealt with.

It all began when my husband told me about a video he'd watched about bear safety. This came shortly before we left on our vacation to Yellowstone and Glacier National Parks. While I appreciated his cautionary information about what to do if you encounter a bear, just hearing it caused old fears to raise their ugly head. I found myself worrying about it frequently and was constantly on guard. I would envision different scenarios of facing a wild bear and what I'd do if it happened. *Raise your arms up high and make yourself look bigger, make loud grunting noises and whatever you do, don't run,* I told myself each time.

The pervading fear that clung to me likely stemmed from two recent and terrifying dog attacks that I'd experienced. One happened only a few months prior to our vacation. After both attacks, I was left with a sense of fear and vulnerability that was hard to shake. When I had the experience of the troubled teenager attacking from behind as described in my closet vision, anxiety plagued me for years afterward. After that incident, I'd suffered anxiety whenever anyone came up behind me. Therapists say that it is normal to have fears of this nature after a traumatic experience. Two new incidents now added an uncertain sense of safety. However, as a believer and one to whom God had clearly revealed His protection over the years, I knew it wasn't right or good for me to have such doubts and fears. *God has always been there for me and protected me from grave harm—why should I have fearful thoughts,* I reassured myself. Still, this fear invaded my spiritual armor with nagging annoyance.

Both dog attacks happened while walking my dog in my neighborhood. With the first attack, I was also walking a neighbor's dog when a huge Mastiff charged out of his unlatched gate and began attacking this dog. When the second attack happened with two dogs (a pit bull and Great Dane) that suddenly came out of a different neighbor's yard, it was déjà vu. But this time, the pit bull viciously attacked my little Maltipoo.

"Why, Lord, why?" I had cried out, as I walked back home, carrying my wounded little dog, both of us trembling. "I can't believe you let this happen again!"

Thankfully, my dog survived and I wasn't physically harmed. After the incidents happened, I found myself fearful for weeks, even months, and my devotional walking time was threatened. I tried to be thankful and focus on the fact that the dogs did not attack me. Yet, these two attacks, coupled with the history of the personal attack years ago, added a new layer of fear to my apprehension regarding the remote possibility of a bear attack.

After two fun-filled weeks and no bear sightings, we chose to travel one more time up the "Going to The Sun Road" in Glacier National Park. My husband Larry and I were awestruck with the beauty God displays there. His creation wraps itself around every bend in the road and spills down every waterfall, into rivers and lakes below. The mountains are God's most awesome and majestic diamonds on display. Ascending up these gargantuan creations filled my soul with the wonder of God's amazing creative facets and left little room for lingering doubts or fears.

As we neared the end of this feast for the eyes, a spray of wildflowers sprinkled their color across meadows alongside. God had seemingly heard my silent yearning and added this final touch that completed our visual eye candy. Up until that point, flowers had been pretty scarce. We pulled over at the next turnout and I got out. While Larry waited in the car, I walked about ten to fifteen feet away, looking at various views through my camera lens, seeking the best shot. I spotted a rounded brown bulge, in stark contrast to the grasses, about thirty or forty feet away. *Hmmm. I wonder what that is,* I thought to myself. *Maybe it's an animal. Probably a deer.* It raised its head. A-a-ah, it's a-a-a *bear!* Dashing with Olympic speed, I ran back to the car and jumped in. The bear had not spotted me yet, but as I slammed the car door, I saw him coming towards our car! Whew! He came within ten feet of the safety of the locked car. I frantically shot photos with lightning speed.

Wow, that was a close one! Mulling over my action, I realized I hadn't reacted in ways I'd planned. I'd done exactly the opposite—I ran! Yet it was the best reaction, as the car was the safest place. Also, when I spotted the bear, he was looking away. Other tourists were pulled over, taking photos and having the bear's attention. It annoyed me that none of them had warned me as I got out of the car and walked into danger. They must have assumed I saw the bear and being blonde had filtered out all reason. I assumed they were all taking photos of wildflowers like me. Funny how we tend to project our motives onto others. One guy, who looked deceptively bright, never did get back in his car, but I was able to find safety in time. My Lord had protected me from danger again. How could I ever doubt Him? Ironically, one of the photos I shot was magazine-worthy, as the bear stood beautifully adorned with blue lupine in the foreground. I got my photo of wildflowers after all, with an added bonus, too.

Meanwhile, back at the ranch, I pondered my close encounter. Sadly, only five days after our return home, there was a news report of a park ranger being mauled to death by a grizzly in Glacier National Park. He most certainly knew all the correct ways to handle a bear encounter, so I was mystified. I prayed for him and his family, knowing the tragic loss it must be to them.

Two weeks after our return, I attended a Bible study entitled: The Armor of God, by Phyllis Shirer. As we discussed our homework and the new insights God's Word had brought us, something occurred to me. Though there are physical dangers lurking in our world, the most dangerous enemy is the one we can't see. I saw that I needed to pray more diligently for protection from the devil's deadly and dangerous schemes rather than just physical threats. I needed to "put on the full armor of God," in any case, so that I "may be able to stand against the wiles of the devil" (Ephesians 6:10 NKJ).

There may come a day when something terrible, even deadly, will happen to me, like the horrible attack that took the park ranger's life. However, once again my Lord has chosen to preserve me. At home the next day, I opened God's Word to a verse I was familiar with: "For God has not given us a spirit of fear, but of power and of love and of sound mind" (2 Timothy 1:7 NKJ).

Purple to the Rescue

The virtuous woman as described in Proverbs 31 is commonly set forth as a standard for Christian women and has always been a favorite of mine. While I fall sorely behind in meeting that standard in many ways, especially the part about rising before dawn, one characteristic is especially fitting for me—the love of the color purple. Long before I became a woman, purple was my favorite color. In fact, it actually came to my rescue once, saving me from a bully.

For me the middle school years—junior high, as we called it then, were the most tumultuous part of growing up. Dealing with the daunting new responsibility of several classes, remembering locker combinations and battling emerging hormones was a walk in the park next to the stress of peer pressures. To say I was a scrawny little kid was putting it kindly. Those of us who hadn't yet caught up with the leaders of the pack—the already well-endowed, beautiful and popular girls—faced a double dose of intimidation. Just about the time I felt secure in finding a best friend, another friend stepped in with divisive betrayal. They both turned against me with cutting and hurtful words that pierced deep into my spirit. So when a bully began taunting me too, it was almost more than I could handle.

Bullies didn't just appear in the 21st century, they've been around a long time and mine was the girl who happened to have a locker next to mine in P.E. One of the other dreaded experiences of middle school was the embarrassing predicament of changing clothes and showering next to strangers. These revealing close quarters apparently ignited a rage of hatred towards me that was without merit. Every opportunity she had, this bully would taunt and intimidate me. One such day caught me "up-to-here" with her ugly threats.

I got in her face and told her if she didn't stop bothering me, she would be sorry because, "I know karate." Of course it was an unfounded threat. A bluff. About all I knew regarding karate was what I'd seen in movies and television. She immediately called my bluff.

"Oh yeah! What color belt do you have?" she challenged me.

My mind scrambled furiously for the right response to the proverbial punch she threw my way. (Apparently there are multiple belt colors—who knew, back then?)

"Purple," I shouted back with false bravado, while praying that belt color even existed in karate.

Turning from raging red to ghostly pale, the bully's face revealed my well-placed blow had hit square on. She shrank back in retreat. Apparently, I'd chosen just the right color level—not too high, not too low—to be a convincing foe.

The bully girl in the locker room never bothered me again. So that was the day the color purple came to my rescue. Now, years later as a grown woman, I see in Proverbs 31:22b and 24 that the virtuous woman "is clothed in fine linen and purple" also, she "makes linen garments and sells them, and supplies sashes for the merchants." In verse 25 it goes on to say, "strength and honor are her clothing." A sash is a kind of belt typically worn in Biblical days. How ironic I thought, as this scripture spoke to me today in new ways. I also wonder if the belts she provided for the merchants gave them a sense of confidence and strength as they faced the challenges of the marketplace while selling their wares. Some of them may have been purple, too.

Ephesians 6:11-14 affirms that the underlying true belt that girds us against the enemy is God's word. "Put on the whole armor of God, that you may be able to stand against the wiles of the devil....Stand therefore, having girded your waist with truth..." As we go out into this world today, it grows increasingly important that we put the *belt of truth* around our waist, because we never know what kind of devilish bully may challenge us.

Rain Upon Iron

Like rain upon iron,
Rejection produces rust.
And injustice withers the spirit,
If in you, we do not trust.

Temper me like steel, oh Lord.
Let my soul become wise.
Bring your mercies to my door,
And justice to my eyes.

Open the visions of my soul,
To the working of your hand.
Let it see your perfect will,
And only on you, stand.

Rejection once rained on you,
And still it does today.
Injustice tried to conquer too,
But redemption had its way.

You were despised and betrayed.
Great sorrow yet embraced.
And so much more,
You suffered for,
To bring us all your grace.

By Iris Carignan, 2015

Chapter 2

His Surprising Joy

Unexpected Laughter

Solomon certainly expressed the joyful essence of laughter in his proverb, "A merry heart makes a cheerful countenance." They say that in comedy, timing is everything. Being a bit of a comedienne myself, I have also found that the element of surprise is equally important to soliciting a laugh. The best set-up is when you don't see it coming, when you don't expect the punch line or the outcome of a tale.

It was that kind of a surprising moment one morning when my Lord made me laugh. I was simply leaving after the church service ended and was ruminating on the size of our new congregation. Having just transitioned from a small church to one with an attendance in the thousands had been quite an adjustment for me. The throngs of people that morning overwhelmed me with a sense of insignificance, loss and even loneliness. We had invested so much energy, time and faith in the former church body, yet we had clearly felt His leading to this new community of believers. Then, as I made my way through the mass of people, the struggle within me evoked an examining conversation with God.

I told Him: *I really love it here, but I just don't know if I can get used to all these people.*

It was then that I heard Him say to me (not audibly, of course), *Then what are you going to do when you get to heaven?*

"Oh," I exclaimed aloud, looked up and laughed at this unexpected and humorous response from my Lord. I knew then that He would carry me through this rough patch and I was determined to persevere. So God made me laugh with His well-timed words.

We stuck it out and found great fellowship with many new Christian brothers and sisters. We learned that the key to not feeling lost in the crowd was to join one of the church's many small groups. God continues to bless the church and the attendance has now grown to more than twice its previous size. Regardless of the number of people I find myself surrounded by, I no longer feel like a stranger or "foreigner," but as a "fellow citizen with God's people and member of God's household." For "God has made me laugh" (Genesis 21:6 NKJ).

Unexpected Smile

Have you ever felt God smile? Well, there was a day when I did. I know that sounds pretty weird, but that is exactly what happened. I *felt* God smile. It all started with a prayer for our daughter. It was in February of 2002 and I had just finished one of many prayers for my daughter. Like all of our children, I had been praying since her early teens that the Lord would prepare the person whom she would marry. By this date she had reached her mid-twenties and my list of requested qualities had grown along with a little anxiousness. Then, just after that prayer, I felt the most unexpected and interesting impression of God smiling.

Smiling back, I took that to mean that this would be the year she would meet Mr. Right.

In respect for my daughter's adult independence and privacy, I didn't mention any of this to her, but waited patiently to hear about anyone special in her life. It wasn't until about eight months later that she called one night and gently began telling me of someone who had become special to her. I listened with growing excitement, knowing full well where the conversation was going. Sure enough, my daughter told me she was in love. She went on to tell me about all his wonderful qualities. I thought of my list as she waxed on in excitement. "He is a doctor" (intelligent: check), "a Christian" (believer: check), "he loves to dance" (common hobbies: check) and on and on.

I could also hear a little anxiousness growing in her voice and sensed that there was something she hadn't yet mentioned. Then she told me that the man she loved was also a black man. That was when I finally knew why God had smiled that day several months before. He knew that this would be an adjustment for me. I was born in the South, and though I never thought of myself as prejudiced and abhorred those who demonstrated it, the idea of one of my children marrying someone of another race had never entered my mind. It certainly wasn't part of my "list" for God. That had to be why I had felt Him smile. That was when the smile that had stirred within my heart for months bubbled up into an effervescent laugh full of realization. God had answered my prayers and I knew that this young man would be the perfect answer to my prayers for our daughter. He did indeed "smile on me and teach me the right way to live" (Psalm 119:135, The Message). They have been happily married for several years now and we continue to rejoice in their union made in heaven. Two gorgeous granddaughters became an added bonus too.

God's Comedic Timing and Precious Gifts

We often laugh in response to the unexpected and that is what happened when Sarah, at the age of about ninety, heard the angel of God promise Abraham that she was going to "bring forth a child even in her old age" (Genesis 18:10–15). Although we are told that "she laughed silently to herself from inside the tent," apparently it was within supernatural earshot of the angelic visitors that day. It was her first recorded laugh. Then, about a year later, just as the angel promised, she gave birth to the child and again her laughter was recorded.

We don't know how many years had transpired between the first patriarchal promise given to Abraham in Genesis 15:5 and the joyous events of fulfillment occurred. We can only imagine that Sarah was fully aware of this prophetic hope from the beginning and that she too had clung on with weakening strength. So, after approximately seventy years of waiting for the realization of God's promise, it was likely that Sarah's hope had dimmed significantly. God's message certainly came at an unexpected time in her journey of faith. I think she might agree that God's timing went well beyond the typical comedic necessity, but it did indeed evoke historical laughter and, in fact, the name Isaac means "laughter."

The story of Abraham and Sarah, and the laughter it evoked, brings to mind one of my own favorite pregnancy stories. Not long after getting my first job as a grocery store cashier, my manager asked me to be the store Easter bunny. It seems that I was the only employee who could fit into their costume. I was happy to comply with this fun request. Then, four years into my bunny hopping role and three years into marriage, I was seven months pregnant with my first child, so the costume barely fit. About two weeks after my last bunny hop through the store, one of my regular customers came in and shared something her kids had said. Apparently these small children recognized me as the Easter bunny even with my regular store uniform on and also noticed that my tummy was quite large. They wanted to know why the Easter bunny had such a big stomach. The mother had then told them that I was going to have a baby. That's when she said "they couldn't wait to see the baby bunnies!" Of course, we both had a good belly laugh from that one.

Not all pregnancies, whether expected or unexpected, bring laughter. Imagine how hard Sarah's pregnancy must have been at such an advanced age. Think about the difficulty and shame experienced by Mary when she was found to be with child out of wedlock. Now think about the fact that Abraham and Sarah were the first family in the genealogy of Jesus Christ and Mary became the mother of Jesus. The Lord chose these two women to be part of His special plan and His timing made both pregnancies extraordinary. Visualize what our world would be if either of these faith-filled women had not trusted the Lord in their circumstances.

Most pregnancies are not as significant as these were, but all babies are miraculous gifts of God and can bring a lot of joy and laughter. Psalm 127:3 (NLT) puts it this way: "Children are a gift from the Lord."

Blessed Joy

In 1997 we welcomed our first grandchild—a baby boy named Christian. While I was looking forward to this new baby, I really didn't know just how joyful it would be until it happened. His mother, my daughter-in-law, had a laborious delivery and I was eager to assist when it was time for her to come home from the hospital. Her doctor, unfortunately, had rushed her out of the recovery with only two days rest from the surgical birth. Knowing she couldn't avoid two flights of stairs to their apartment, I begged the doctor to let her stay in the hospital longer, but without success, probably due to insurance issues. Needless to say, she was exhausted and in pain upon arriving home. But I know that my son and his wife were full of joy at the birth of their first child, as I had been with his birth. This son who had my first grandchild was also my first child.

They say that childbirth is one of the most painful experiences a person can have and I agree, having given birth to three children myself. All three of my babies weighed over eight pounds, even though I was tiny. My last baby was such a long and arduous birth that I fainted immediately afterwards. However, the pain was quickly forgotten as I held those precious gifts in my arms. Then, a swift twenty-five years later, I had the special joy of holding a grandchild. When my son and his wife asked me to babysit him for the first time, my joy was still overflowing. With a rocking motion to calm him, I paced the floor and my joy spilled over into a new lullaby song. "Weeping may remain for the night, but rejoicing comes in the morning" (Psalm 30:5b).

You may even have the privilege of cradling the next generation of your little miracles and joyfully respond with an inspired lullaby. I now have seven grandchildren and rejoice in such great blessing. Each new grandbaby was held and rocked to sleep with that same inspired lullaby song "What the Angel's See". I am also proud and happy to say that today that first grandchild is a healthy young man named Christian, who also loves the Lord and honors Jesus with his walk, not just his name.

What the Angels See

Roses and bows,
Butterflies and toads,
These are the things that a baby sees.

Soft whispered breeze,
Kisses on the knees,
Tell of the love that they know.

Bend down to see what the angels see,
Soft teddy bears and music for their ears.
God blesses all the babies with these things.
So don't miss the joy that a baby brings.

Time passes by,
Little babies fly,
Into the world of the grown.
But you can relive
The blessings that they give,
When they've a child of their own.

Bend down to see what the angels see,
Soft teddy bears and music for their ears.
God blesses all the babies with these things.
So don't miss the joy that a baby brings

God blesses all the babies with these things,
So don't miss the joy that a baby brings.

Music and lyrics by Iris Carignan, 1994

Surprising Fun on Cue

One of my favorite vacation stories happened the year we decided to travel to Disney World and Epcot Center in Florida. Because I mostly grew up in Southern California, I had been to Disneyland many times, but the rumor was that Disney World was better. Well, those rumors not only proved to be wrong, but our pass to the Magic Kingdom in Florida and Epcot Center came packaged in the most oppressively humid heat I've ever experienced. We also found that this amusement park version was missing some of our favorite rides and the ones that were there didn't seem as exciting. Mostly, this travel-weary bunch of Californians just couldn't handle the muggy weather that dragged us down and threatened to spoil the whole vacation. Nevertheless, we had paid our money, so we were "going to have fun, even if it killed us!" At some point, our daughter brightened and said, "I know, let's go on the Pirates of the Caribbean ride." It was our favorite and figured it might bring some excitement to our day (not to mention it was usually cool inside). With drummed up enthusiasm, she and I raced ahead of my husband, Larry, and our son to get there first.

Having arrived well before the guys, we were about ten or eleven people ahead of them in line. The rippling rise of heat seemed to waver with more intensity and distort our spirits like a carnival mirror as we slowly moved closer to the ride entrance. Making matters even more unbearable, just behind me was a loud-mouthed bore that began telling me his whole life story. He seemed almost too fittingly like an exaggerated cartoon character from one of Disney's stories. The queue continued its typical slow cattle style snaking back and forth toward the ride entrance when I spotted Larry and our son approaching us from the other side of the dividing bar. Up until this point, we hadn't said a word to each other and it was likely that no one even knew

25

we were together. On impulse, I suddenly reached across the aisle, grabbed Larry (my husband) around the neck and said, "Hi cutie!" and planted a big kiss on his mouth.

The blockhead behind me must have nearly lost his lunch. I'm quite sure his big mouth extended to its fullest drop-down position before he blurted out "Whoa, buddy, you must have done something right!"

It was all I could do not to burst out laughing, but I turned and proceeded forward as if I didn't know the man I'd just lip-locked.

The rest of our day at Disney World seemed to fly by with exuberance like never before experienced at any amusement park. Even the oppressive heat seemed to dissipate into the air of our imaginative spontaneity. Perhaps Disney World did have an extra dose of magic there. It was the biggest highlight of the day and by far topped the charts of our vacation experiences.

James 1:17 (NIV) says: "Every good and perfect gift is from above, coming down from the Father of the heavenly lights." This may not have been a spiritual gift as intended in this verse, but it certainly was the perfect gift for us that day. In a world filled with all kinds of discomforts and trials much worse than a hot humid day, we can always look for joyful opportunities. If we aren't able to see it with humor or new vision despite our valiant efforts, we know that we should continue to praise the Lord regardless. 1 Thessalonians 5:18 (NIV) says it best: "Give thanks in all circumstances, for this is God's will for you in Christ Jesus."

Unexpected Joy

Easter will be here again before we know it. Hallelujah! We'll sing praises to our Lord and Savior who gave the ultimate sacrifice for us and demonstrated His holiness by rising from the grave. We can shout and sing for joy at this amazing miracle and His grace as we consider the cross in retrospect. However, just days before our Savior's resurrection, things were desperately sorrowful to all who loved Him. This verse shows that even Jesus needed to see beyond the immediate suffering and look to the joy that lay ahead.

God showed me this lesson when I had to undergo a couple of cardiac tests to determine any problems that may have caused a fainting spell. It had occurred while attending a women's Bible study and the incident had been a little disconcerting and troubling for sure. As I lay there on the floor of our church, half conscious, I could hear the paramedics proclaiming that they couldn't get a reading after taking my blood pressure. A few more tries didn't seem to work either. Friends had gathered around me when it all started and did their best to make me comfortable until the ambulance had arrived.

I sensed their worry at hearing the concerned comments by my attendants, and began to feel a little anxious myself. Could it be that this was more serious than it seemed? Silently I prayed and thanked God for all the many blessings He had poured onto me through the years. Feeling at peace even during the turmoil, I did my best to calm the men who had carefully placed me in the ambulance by telling them one of my favorite jokes. My blood pressure finally rose to a level that was measurable and we all relaxed a little.

One week later, I was undergoing the second of two cardiac tests. The morning of this test, I opened the Bible and read: "Let us fix our eyes on Jesus, the author and finisher of our faith, who for the joy set before him endured the cross" (Hebrews 12:2 NKJ). The lady administering the test was friendly, and early into the process, she turned our conversation toward God. She began telling me how God had protected her and her family during many times of crises. We seemed to have much in common, yet I sensed that she was of a different faith. I also began sharing some of the times the Lord had protected me, and that I was writing a book about them. Other applicable scriptures popped clearly into my head and I was able to share them as well, but mostly I listened to her.

At some point, the verse given me that morning seemed to fit perfectly, so I mentioned it too. I began sensing a more "holy" reason for this medical appointment. As things progressed, her comments became more and more proselytizing in nature. Reincarnation entered her dialogue and further on she confirmed my suspicions that she was Hindu. The scripture says: "It is appointed for men to die once" (Hebrews 9:27) I said softly. She continued to wax on about all the evidences for her faith and how good it was.

"Do you know there is a core difference between the Christian faith and every other religion in the world?" I asked.

"What is that?" She asked.

"All other faiths teach that it is what a person *does* that determines their eternal fate. The core belief of Christianity," I went on, "says that it's what *God did* for us through Jesus on the cross, *not what we do*, that paved our way to eternal life. All we need to do is accept that gift."

Not fully hearing or understanding at first, she tried to say that they also believe in doing good things. "No." I repeated, "It isn't by doing good deeds, it isn't by being good or trying hard. No matter how hard we try we will never be as good as God and that is why the only perfect person, Jesus, had to pay the price for us. What He did on the cross that day is what makes it possible for us to have eternal life, not anything we do. Jesus suffered a terrible death and yet because He knew of the joy that would come of it He was able to face it."

My cardiac test was finished. Bringing myself to a sitting position and facing her directly, I asked if she knew that Jesus also said, "You must be born again?"

"No," she said in amazement.

"Yes, what He meant," I went on to explain, "is that we are all born in the natural way of flesh, but, when we come to a place where we accept His sacrifice for us and believe that He died and rose for our sins, then we receive His Holy Spirit and are born spiritually."

Exiting the exam room, I thanked my new friend and she said she wanted to read my book when it was finished. God had given me a joyous verse for the day. If I had known that He would use the stressful incident of fainting to bring someone else closer to God, no doubt I would have been even more at peace and full of joy while lying on the floor of my church that day. It wasn't until much later when it occurred to me that I had hardly noticed the discomfort of the exam. In truth it was clear to me that God's Spirit and leading that day had filled the hour with joy.

The Troubadour's Song

When the sun begins to shine in Troubadour,
Life begins again
Birds begin to sing outside your door,
And love comes shining in
Truth may not find a way,
So many things to coax and sway

Our hearts will only love,
When we give place to
The light from above.
And surrender all that we adore,
Then we become troubadours.

By Iris Carignan, 2008

Gracious Joy and the Heavy Stone

At the young age of nine I asked Jesus to be my Savior. Life was pretty simple then, but fifteen years later, happily married with a family and church responsibilities, I found myself more and more stressed. *What's wrong with me*—noting the shakiness in my young hands. That shakiness continued day after day, no matter how much I prayed and tried to seek peace. Finally, after several months of frustration with this nervous *"imperfection,"* I called my pastor and asked for counsel. We talked for quite a while and I poured out my emotional turmoil at what I perceived to be my flaws. In my own mind, this nervous shaking was a symptom of an imperfection that should not be present in a Christian. After all, I was active in church and tried hard to be a good wife and mother and an overall *good person.*

My pastor softly and lovingly spoke grace into my heart by telling me that Jesus loves me just the way I am. I didn't have to earn His love. That simple phrase struck home with unexpected precision.

After he left, I knelt down on the floor of my bedroom and poured out my heart to the Lord as never before. In those moments, God revealed to me that striving for perfection was actually prideful sin. I realized that I was trying to earn God's love by doing anything and everything the church asked me to do. Then, the most amazing feeling of lightness and peace came over me, accompanied by the sensation of a very heavy load lifting off my body. I felt fifty pounds lighter and at only 103 pounds, that was remarkable! I was overtaken by joy like never before. I knew then that Jesus had taken the weight of works off my shoulders and replaced it with His grace. Up to that point in my Christian life, the message of grace had reached my ears, but not my heart.

It has been years since that day of spiritual rebirth, and sometimes I fall back into worldly striving. Coincidentally, it's usually during those times that the joy of the Lord slips away too. Gently He reminds me of His grace. Easter is our best confirmation that His sacrifice rolled away the heavy stone of self-righteousness and the sin that separates. "For by grace you have been saved through faith, and that not of yourselves; it is the gift of God, not of works, lest anyone should boast" (Ephesians 2:8 NKJ).

The Greatest Joy

The greatest joy is to come alone
To the Lord of Hosts
Who removed the stone.

And the greatest peace can be found in prayer
When you come to Him in solitaire.

For He comes to those who abide in Him
And He rolls the stone
Away from sin.

By Iris Carignan

Chapter 3

Open Ears to Hear

His Distinctive Voice

Early in my career as an artist, I had the privilege of joining a fellow artist to get photographs of some sheep grazing at lambing time. My friend is an accomplished Christian artist who was working on a Good Shepherd painting series and needed some reference photos. She had befriended a local shepherd and asked permission to go in amongst the sheep. I had seen sheep before, even had them grazing on a field near our first home, but this was far more intimate and gave me new insights regarding this common animal. More than a lesson in animal husbandry, it opened my eyes and ears to why sheep were often used to illustrate principals in the Bible.

As we began walking the hills and taking photographs, I became aware of an unexpected chorus of bleating. It struck me that the sheep all had different voice ranges. Some sheep had what I would call alto voices, some soprano, bass, and so on. They were clearly sheep voices, but each seemed distinctive to the individual sheep. Then I heard a large adult sheep up on a hillside, bleating continuously. There was a sudden stirring nearby and I watched as a little lamb scrambled up the hill to its mother.

She had been calling for her lamb to nurse and he obviously recognized her voice. It hit me that these simple yet wonderful creatures clearly recognized the distinct voices of each other as well as the voice of their shepherd. No wonder our Lord used this commonly known fact to illustrate that we should recognize His voice too. In John 10:27 we read, "My sheep hear my voice and I know them and they follow me." And again in: John 10:4 "And when he brings out his own sheep, he goes before them; and the sheep follow him, for they know his voice."

I don't recall my friend noticing the variation in tone of the sheep and no doubt she was focusing on her goal for the day. How often, I wonder, do I get so focused on my own goals, that I miss the voice of the Lord? The Lord's voice is a distinct kind of voice that is more real and awesome than any I've heard audibly. Before the fall of man and the casting of Adam and Eve out of the Garden of Eden, there was a more direct communion with God. There was no doubt in their minds who was talking when He spoke. Yet even they were willing to follow another voice with great and historic consequence to all of humanity.

Hearing and recognizing the Lord's voice is the first step towards a more fruitful life. Feeding on the Shepherd's word nourishes our souls with eternal food. Following the right voice is imperative in our quest to honor our Good Shepherd.

An Urgent Nudge and Unexpected Turn

It was the summer of 2001 and I was scurrying around in final preparation for an art show. Normally, my husband Larry would have also been helping, but he was on a well-deserved men's retreat in Nevada. Most of the art festivals I do are a lot of work and require extra muscle to get everything loaded and set up, but this one was a small local show and a more manageable one.

After loading the truck, I showered and mentally reviewed my checklist of things to bring. A sudden and clear thought streamed into my mind as if the shower had cleansed me of anxiousness and replaced it with a more pressing need. *Pray for Larry*, it prompted. A vague thought of something happening to him in water seemed to couple the nudge. Okay, I promised, as soon as I finish my shower (as if God couldn't hear me in there).

Gulping down another sip of coffee and grabbing the final small items I needed for the show, I started toward the door. *Pray for Larry*, the thought came back. Oh yeah, I forgot to do that! I sat down immediately and began praying for my husband as another thought that something was going to happen to him in the water whispered in the recesses of my mind again. It was probably just my own worrywart tendency, I reasoned, and dashed out the door with confidence that my Lord had it covered.

My art display was all set up and the show just getting started. A friend and fellow artist was set up with her paintings right next to mine. The weather was beautiful and I was glad to have her close by to share in the prospects of good sales. Then my cell phone rang. It was my daughter-in-law with news that something had happened to Larry. With guarded caution, she went on to explain that there had been an accident while he was on a Jet Ski in the lake. My oldest son, Jason, had also been involved in the accident, but seemed to be okay. In shock, I turned to my friend to sort out what to do next.

Within a few short hours, my son Gavin beside me on the plane and my daughter, Ivy, at home prayerfully taking care of other matters, I flew to my husband's side. *Oh Lord, please don't let him have any internal bleeding or head injuries.* Jason met us at the airport and filled in some of the details of the accident as we drove to the hospital. We learned that he had accidentally run over his dad with the Jet Ski he was on. Jet Skis do not have brakes; their speed is controlled only by a gas pedal, so when my husband unexpectedly turned his ski into our son's path, there wasn't enough time to stop. Our son had run right over the top of him and knocked him into the water. Thankfully, they both had life vests on and Larry told me that his first thought as he came up and saw Jason's empty Jet Ski was to pray for him. A nearby boater saw the accident and came to the rescue. The boater took Larry to a nearby pier and a helicopter lifted and rushed him to the closest hospital.

We arrived late that night. After many kisses and gentle hugs to his battered body, I stepped into the hospital hall for a brief moment of repose. My head felt woozy and my knees buckled, sending me to the floor in full realization of the seriousness of what had happened. Larry had three broken ribs, a punctured lung, and a pelvis broken in three places, but *no internal bleeding or head injury. Thank you Lord!* It was a long and arduous recovery process and difficult for both Larry and I, but thankfully God had saved him from any grave injuries and protected our son from harm, too.

After that day, I will never forget the importance of heeding a prod to prayer and I continue to praise God for his mercy in all of this. He had nudged me to pray for my husband that morning and I got so caught up in the worries of the day, that I nearly missed praying for a more urgent and important matter.

"And take the helmet of salvation...praying always with all prayer and supplication in the Spirit..." (Ephesians 6:17–18).

Inspirations of the Master

When is the last time you took a quiet stroll and observed creation all around you? Did you praise your Lord and creator as you walked and listened to His still and quiet voice? Perhaps, instead, you were bent over a cell phone, trying to catch up on some business calls? Did you listen to the birds sing and chirp their joyful morning song and realize they know enough to praise their creator even with their limited intelligence? Has their song lifted your spirit with new hope?

I have a little dog that looks forward to his walk with eager tail-wagging excitement each day. This daily ritual is one that I have grown to love too. It has become a quiet time to walk and talk with the Lord. Often while walking and communing with Him, He will speak to me in poetic phrases. I must admit, though, sometimes other pressing matters snatch away that special joy before we take the first step out the door. I just want to get the walk over. My schedule may be especially full or perhaps the weather isn't so good. My dog, however, always wants to go out and seems sad if it gets delayed too long. It occurs to me that I should be more like my canine friend, always anxious for the good walk and thankful for the opportunity to remove myself from my environment of phone calls, jobs to do and every other kind of distraction. This, I remind myself, is the most important part of today's journey. After all, didn't someone once say that the most important part of any journey is the first step?

Having a devotional walk on my street also provides many opportunities to meet and greet my neighbors. Sometimes it gives me the chance to learn of a need or joy one of them may have. These walks are truly a gift for each new day and I thank my Lord that I have the health and ability to do it.

The next chance you get to take a walk, remember to look up at His beautiful sky and praise Him for "The heavens proclaim the glory of God. The skies display the work of his hands" (Psalm 19:1). Look ahead and praise Him for what He has planned for your day. Look at your neighbors' houses and pray for them. Listen to the sounds of His creation all around you and let His voice speak through them to you.

And Men Also To Sing

Oh Lord who made the birds to fly
And men also to sing,
You made the mountains rise up to sky
And water fall down to springs.

You caused the darkness of the night
And brought the morning dew
To calm the angry roar of life
And help us think of you.

And when I hear your voice
In whispers through the trees,
It carries my spirit to a place
Of praises on my knees.
Why does my heart still yearn for more?

When all creation around
Speaks so loudly of your love
With beauty and with sound
And nature's miracles both great and small
All bowed to the greatest miracle of all.

For you showed the world your love
By sending Jesus from above.
And nature's ways were conquered that day
When from the grave you rose to stay.

So praise the wonders of His love,
Let all creation bring
Thanksgiving to our God
And men also to sing!

Iris Carignan, 2011

Surprising Language

Early in my adult walk with the Lord, I had a yearning to receive
the gift of tongues. Many of my daily prayers would seek after
this gift. It seemed to be such a powerful sign and confirmation
of being filled with His Holy Spirit as demonstrated also in the
book of Acts. More than that, I naively wished to be able to speak
in another language so that I might be able to evangelize people
of foreign lands. Alas, after about a year of pleading for this gift,
I saw no sign of it. It wasn't until about twenty years later that I
had a "tongue" experience.

We had only recently joined the new large non-denominational
church where we are now active members, when I experienced
the Holy Spirit speaking to me in another language. During
a dinner honoring the many missionaries we send from our

congregation, we were all bowed in prayer for the fourth couple presenting information about their ministry in Europe, when it began. I heard the sound of French being spoken. It wasn't an audible kind of sound, but it was clearly like hundreds of people speaking French all at once. I never studied French, but knew enough about how it sounded to recognize it as such. Realizing I was the only one hearing this caused me to wonder what it meant. The prayer of the leader continued and the collective cacophony of voices in my head prompted silent prayers for an explanation. Are you trying to tell me something, Lord? If you are trying to send me a message in another language, I need to hear the words more distinctly. Just after that prayer went up, I began to hear an individual voice speaking one word in what sounded like French, over and over several times. Then, as if knowing that I got it, another word, also in French, began repeating over and over in my head. There seemed to be one more word that came quickly between the two, but I wasn't so sure I caught that one clearly.

After prayer ended, I sat in stunned silence, pondering what had just happened and if it had any true meaning. Was I going crazy or was it real? Was it truly the sound of French and had meaning or just a bunch of gobbledygook? The last missionary finished speaking and we were all invited to visit with the folks who had just spoken and to lend our support. Saying nothing to my husband or anyone else, I rose to go speak to one of the missionaries whose area of ministry was in Europe, and especially France. I waited nervously until everyone else had finished talking to him and then asked anxiously if the phrase I'd just heard meant anything. The phrase was Je suis en comprar.

"Yes," said the man. "It does mean something. Translated, it says: I am working alongside you for the same purpose."

I could barely believe what had just happened. God not only gave me a word in another tongue, it was a real language and was relevant to someone. After explaining to the missionary that I had heard the phrase while praying, yet didn't speak French, I returned to my seat, my heart still in my throat. This strange experience preoccupied me with wonder for months. During this time, I had an art student from France who spoke the language fluently. I told this non-believer about the experience and she said it was odd for me to hear the phrase, saying that it is mostly a cultural expression used only in France.

It was only a year ago (about twenty-four years after the incident) that I was able to get the proper spelling written down for me. One of my neighbors is French and I had the opportunity to share the same story with him. He confirmed the interpretation and also gave me the spelling of the phrase. He also explained why I didn't hear the middle part "en" clearly. He said that it was because in properly speaking that phrase the word "en" gets joined in a kind of slur of words together and isn't supposed to be distinctive.

There haven't been any additional such tongue experiences for me since that day, twenty-four plus years ago, but whenever I remember it, my heart is blessed with a confirmation of God's reassurance to others through His voice. It was clearly a word given to me for the encouragement of my Christian brother, the missionary to Europe, but it confirmed my faith as well. God's word also clearly teaches that when He speaks to his children, it is always for the purpose of bringing glory to Him, not for our edification. God knew that that missionary needed to hear a word of encouragement and so did I. He gracefully chose to glorify His name in an unexpected way that blessed us both that day.

An Unexpected Kiss

Like the harmony that you hear
Inside your mind's ear,
Is the voice that He does whisper,
To the song of your heart so clear.

With sweet surprise
The thought arrives,
Not wanting to be missed.
A message He gives,
Like an unexpected kiss.

So listen close and don't deny,
When His melodious word
Is given by and by.

He is the author of everyone's song
The composer of your life.
And He knows of every joy
And of every strife.

He hits the high notes and the low,
Every place your heart song goes.
And placing the notes of each measure
Into proper time,
His voice with ours, together,
Can bring harmony, rhythm and rhyme.

Iris Carignan, 2015

Josie's Story—"God Speaks and I Listen"

"Lord, what took you so long?" The pleading question poured from Josie's heart that day in 1979. "That was when God first spoke to me," she began. About nine years earlier she had turned her life over to God, and every day since, she had begged Him to release her from a dark secret—alcoholism and addiction. Now after four months of sobriety, she asked her Lord why it had taken so long. Why hadn't He just removed the strong temptation that dogged her daily? Why did she have to join Alcoholics Anonymous to get sober? Why didn't He heal her from this terrible "thorn in the flesh" (2 Corinthians 12:7 NKJ) on the very day she had become a believer? But the day came when she unexpectedly heard His response to those nagging questions. She heard God say that she needed to be with people who shared the same issues, so that she would know she wasn't alone in her addictions.

The first meeting of A.A. that my friend attended became the last day she ever took a drink again, but it hadn't been easy for her to go. Another friend had confided to Josie that both of her parents were alcoholics and how A.A. meetings had helped them. "But what if I see someone there that I know," she protested anxiously, knowing that her secret would be out. She already faced a daily dose of shame every time she peered into a mirror—shame for drinking and shame for what had driven her to drink in the first place. You see, my friend had another secret. She had been molested as a child and while the guilt from it was totally unwarranted, it laid within her soul for years with a stubbornness that refused to leave.

In humble obedience to her Lord, Josie went to the A.A. meeting and with His help and new tools learned in the program, she flourished for several years. That pivotal point of decision placed her feet on a new path of hope and restoration. Then she hit a speed bump that nearly knocked her off course. She and her husband moved to a new community and that meant she couldn't attend the same meeting place. It wasn't long before the baggage of her past reared its head again and she fell into a kind of "funk." Then she remembered what God had said to her and how she realized that He not only heard her plea, He had "led her to the source of help." So she found a new group and got back on track again. This time she began helping others and saw that "It was what I needed—to help others while helping myself."

Many years passed and each one brought new strength through daily communion with the Lord. Her troubling experiences of the past no longer held a power over her, and the spirit of drink was banished; but as with all of us, eventually life brought new challenges. Her husband, Wayne, suffered a series of grave health issues. She struggled with despair, not knowing what to do. It was a different kind of vulnerability that pulled at her now.

"I really didn't know how to pray or what to pray for, but God knew and one day my devotional gave me just the verse I needed."

Opening to Romans 8:26–27 she read: "Likewise the Spirit helps in our time of weakness, for we do not know what we should pray for as we ought, but the Spirit Himself makes intercession for us... Now He who searches the hearts knows what the mind of the Spirit is because He makes intercession for the saints according to the will of God." Not long after that, a friend shared another verse that was especially encouraging to her: "May the God of hope fill you with all joy and peace as you trust in Him, so that you may overflow with hope by the power of the Holy Spirit" (Romans 15:13 NIV).

Her husband passed away, and Josie found herself even more dependent on her Lord. However, a day came when she heard

God speak to her again. She was driving home alone when she noticed a woman walking alongside the road, carrying a load on her shoulders. "I watched as she shifted her shoulders to lighten her burden; God spoke to me and told me to lighten her burden. I felt that He wanted me to stop and offer her a ride." Josie then explained that when she stopped and offered to help the lady, the woman pointed to the next driveway ahead and said that was where she lived. The lady was already at the point of her destination and Josie couldn't understand why God had "clearly" told her to offer a ride.

"Now what was that all about?" She asked God out loud. Later that night, after telling her daughter of the incident, they concluded that maybe the Lord was testing Josie's obedience and perhaps it also was an encouragement to the lady just to have someone offer help.

Josie got past many other troubles in her life that could have caused great destruction, but by then God had taught her much about the value of sharing her heavy burdens with Him and helping others by sharing their burdens. Josie has learned to trust in her Lord and her faith has brought her through the hills and valleys of her journey. No wonder she is more than willing to follow His directive to pull over and lighten the load of a stranger. She also joined Celebrate Recovery, a Christian-based group, which brought new opportunities for her to help others. "His word continues to speak to me in ways that I understand and it's all for His glory that I read it." She goes on to say: "It is when I read scripture out loud that it helps me to listen."

45

Lisa's Unexpected Challenge

Having a beautiful daughter-in-law is a blessing not all are privileged with. My oldest son's wife, Lisa, is such a wonderful example of faith demonstrated. Our son was only twenty-one when he announced his engagement to Lisa. Although he was quite young to be ready for marriage, he was more mature than most for his age and I was thrilled for both of them. It was clear to me that they were right for each other. Yet only recently, and eighteen years into their marriage, she revealed to me how evident God had made it to her.

"I had dated several boys before meeting Jason and the Lord was taking hold of my life," she began. Not coming from a household of faith, so much of Lisa's new journey was especially crucial in laying a good foundation for life, which she recognized early on. She knew how important relationships were to a solid future of walking with the Lord.

Lisa began praying about Jason and asking God's direction regarding their dating and the possibility of their future together. It was during an intense conversation with God that she perceived God had asked her a deep question. *If you were married to Jason and he were to become severely disabled, would you still love him and serve him as his wife the rest of your days?* The challenge came. The reply in her heart was an undeniable yes. The experience confirmed for her a forward commitment to our son.

Ironically, about twelve years into their marriage, it was Lisa, not Jason, who contracted a serious autoimmune disease that is a precursor to Lupus. It's called Undifferentiated Connective Tissue Disorder with Vascular Neuropathy, and has been debilitating to her since. Little did any one of us know that she would be the one to suffer a serious disease, and our son would be called to demonstrate his enduring love for her.

Lisa's battle with this disease continues to be difficult, but the distinct memory of God's challenge that day continues to minister and strengthen her for the battle. Jeremiah 29:1 is especially reassuring to her, Jason, and to their two boys as they serve each other in love and commitment. "For I know the plans I have for you, says the Lord. They are plans for good and not for disaster, to give you a future and a hope" (Jeremiah 29:11).

Unexpected Danger and His Voice

How many of us dream of going to some tropical island and relaxing by beautiful ocean waters? For several years my husband, Larry, and I had listened enviably to friends and relatives talk about their trips to Hawaii and how fabulous it was. I found myself thinking that we might never have the chance to go there. Then one year Larry was asked to consult on a job in Hawaii and we were able to experience that dream. We left our three young children in the capable care of my parents and flew away to paradise. The night before that trip, I had a dream that included the beginning words and music of a new song, "With This Seed". It was an expression of my heart's desire to be a good and fruitful witness for the Lord, and the next morning I was able to pen the whole song given to me in the dream. Surely this would be a blessed and purposeful trip.

The first few days of our trip were spent on business and then we were able to get out and have some fun. On Thursday of that week we decided to do an excursion. We registered for an all day snorkeling and picnic cruise guided by a company named Zodiac Tours. Not being a fan of astrology, I should have taken the name as a warning, but pushed it aside in vain dismissal. We took an hours' boat ride around the island before disembarking on a quiet beach cove for a picnic lunch. After lunch, our guide handed out the snorkeling gear and gave us brief instructions before sending us into the waters.

Being our first experience at snorkeling and not being proficient swimmers, I was a little nervous. We decided it would be a good idea to stick close together. After some initial flustered, gagging attempts, we seemed to have the hang of it. Since we didn't have life vests on, we went into shallow water and quickly learned to use the buoyancy of our bodies to float. The fish were beautiful, but were pretty sparse there, so feeling more confident, we ventured into deeper waters with hopes of spotting more fish. I began swimming back toward shallow water, assuming Larry was still close behind. I turned to see that he was a good distance back and was struggling in the water, so I quickly swam back to him and reached out to grab his arm to help.

Larry had swallowed some water through his snorkel and it had caused him to panic. The more I tried to help, the more he seemed to pull us both down. I let go in fear of drowning with him. It was clear that he was too heavy for this poor swimmer to save. I looked back at the dock where our "life guard" guide was and thought about yelling for help. The guide was facedown asleep on the dock. I began to panic and realized how deep the water was. If I yelled, I thought, it might just make us both panic more and he probably wouldn't hear it anyway, so I began praying for God to help us. He spoke to me and I perceived that He was saying to *stand on the rock*. Dipping down below the surface of the water, I looked around for a rock. There, about four or five feet away, was a giant rock for us to stand on. I told Larry about it and suggested we swim out to it. It took faith to swim into deeper waters, but we did it. The rock was just tall enough so we could hold our heads out of the water, rest awhile and catch our breath.

We made it safely back to shore and sat quietly, thanking God for His help. In embarrassed humility, we neither said anything to our guide. Later that evening, we called Mom to see how the kids were doing. They had tried to call us that day, but because they weren't able to reach us, my mother worried, so they prayed for our safety. A year later, we read in the paper about a couple who drowned while on the same snorkeling excursion.

"The Lord is my rock and my fortress and my deliverer" (Psalm 18:2 NKJ). He truly was our protector and our Rock that day. In this case, He literally "set my feet on a rock and gave me a firm place to stand" (Psalm 40:2). It took a measure of faith and obedience to act on His instruction to "stand on the rock." It meant swimming out into even deeper waters, but I have little doubt about what may have happened if we hadn't. God had spoken to me through the depths of danger and our act of faith and trust became a lesson of great purpose to us. His voice wasn't loud and thunderous that day, but I am so glad I heard it and took action.

Deanna's Unexpected Directive

What about building an orphanage here? That was what Deanna heard that day in Kenya, Africa. Just last year, my husband and I had signed up to sponsor an orphan in Kenya through a ministry called Miracle House. Deanna, the founder of Miracle House, is the daughter of some good friends of ours. We were returning from a business trip when a serendipitous meeting gave me the opportunity to learn more about how she came to establish it.

After finishing our business in Colorado, we were at the Denver airport for a flight back to L.A. As it happens, Deanna lives with her family in the Colorado area and her parents had arranged for her to meet up with all of us at the airport that day. Although Deanna's parents had planned the meeting at the airport for family reasons, I thought it was awfully nice of the Lord to set this up for me. You see, this was the week when I felt He had directed me to include stories from other folks in this book. So while visiting and eating lunch before the flight home, Deanna began sharing her unexpected directive from the Lord.

She was in Kenya, Africa, on an evangelistic mission and had just finished a drama presentation to a large gathering of folks in a slum area of the region. As a result, many had responded to the gospel and became new believers. They connected them with the local pastor, with whom the team had been working, and rejoiced in the harvest of the day. Their work seemed to be done there and the team said their good-byes, but Deanna soon learned the Lord had an even greater mission in mind for her. As they drove away with a sense of accomplishment, the slum they were leaving disappeared in sight, yet clung to their souls. It was on that drive when Deanna heard the voice that was so clear and strong, she had looked around to see who else heard it. Did she really hear God say she was supposed to start an orphanage?

After she arrived back home from that trip, Deanna couldn't stop thinking about the directive. She began praying and asking God if He really wanted her to do that. *"This can't be something you want me to do, Lord,"* she questioned. *"I don't have the proper education or background to do this,"* she argued.

The days, weeks and months that followed brought three clear confirmations to her about this endeavor. Two of the confirmations came while serving in other ministry capacities.

She continued to wrestle with this until one particular confirmation came while sitting in her own dining room. *"I've never really had a heart for ministering to orphans,"* she prayerfully pleaded once more.

The prayer was still fresh in her mind when she glanced to the next room where her two adopted daughters were playing. They were orphans that she and her husband had adopted as babies from Haiti a few years before. "That excuse isn't going to work either, is it?" She said out loud.

Full realization and revelation struck her with clear resonance. When Deanna contacted the same pastor in Kenya to tell him of her wishes to establish an orphanage. "Praise God!" He said. "We have been praying and praying that someone would help us do that." Two years later in 2006, Miracle House was established in that very town of Kenya, Africa. It continues to be an effective ministry to many orphans and a light to the community. Matthew 19:14 says: "Let the little children come to me, and do not forbid them; for of such is the kingdom of heaven."

Wise Counsel

There is an old saying that goes something like this: The man who represents himself in a court of law has a fool for a counselor. In Proverbs 3:7, we read: "Do not be wise in your own eyes." The founding pastor of our church, Larry De Witt, is a wise and honorable man of God. Although he is now retired from full time work as a pastor, he continues to serve through an organization he founded called Cornerstone Ministries. One aspect of his ministry involves giving counsel and comfort to other pastors who serve full time in churches across the nation. He knows full well from experience the many difficulties that can plague a church pastor.

My husband and I remain close to him and when possible, have the blessing of socializing with Pastor Larry and his wife, Beccy. On one particular evening of dinner and fellowship, he shared a recent counseling experience he'd had. He told us of a pastor who was having a few difficulties and differences with his congregation. One of the sticking points was a common one found in many churches today—the music. He had explained that many of his parishioners were constantly complaining that the music was too loud. After a thoughtful pause, Pastor DeWitt said: "Have you considered that maybe the music *is* too loud?"

The pastor went pale with humbled revelation. He knew the counsel he'd been given was right on. It was such a simple and obvious answer; he hadn't even considered it until that moment.

How often do we also fret over something that we can't seem to get over? The matter may ruminate in our minds over and over like a hamster on a wheel. After days or even weeks of circuitous mulling, we find ourselves even more frustrated and angry. *Why can't they just see it my way?* We wonder. When the answer finally comes, it may hit like a bombshell. We realize it was there all along, waiting in simple and obvious terms. Perhaps the question just required someone else's perspective. Maybe we needed to seek wise counsel or sincerely seek God's wisdom through His word. Quite often we mostly needed to listen to God.

The Bible tells us "Blessed is the man who does not walk in the counsel of the wicked or stand in the way of sinners, or sit in the seat of mockers" (Psalm 1:1 NIV). If something is bothering you and no amount of consideration seems to bring a solution, you first need to seek an answer from the Holy Spirit through prayer and from God's word. Second, be careful not to twist and misuse the Bible to suit your own desires. Then, if the matter is not resolved, it may be good to seek counsel. Sometimes that is how God speaks to us. You may not have to seek a paid counselor. Most of us know someone who has proven to be a godly and wise person. Most churches have a pastor or counselor on staff that may be able to help. My go-to person, besides my Lord, is my own husband. After forty-five years of marriage and countless witnesses to his wisdom, I know that I can ask him anything and he will give me good counsel. If it is a matter that we can't resolve, we seek further counsel from a pastor. Praise God that one of the blessings of the church body is access to wise counsel. Now if we can just learn to apply it, we'll do well.

Chapter 4

An Artist's Perspective

An Artist's Recipe for Success

Pick a canvas as big as your goals
To execute with less toil use high quality tools.
Drawing upon the experience of others
Lay out your palette with bright hopeful colors.
Use a forgiving medium generously
And light your subject positively.

Block in the basics with transparent vision
Then stand back and see.
Paint large brushstrokes of faith
And once more stand back and see.

Remember the dark areas accentuate the light
So use criticism sparingly to get it right.
Stir together colors that compliment analogously
And finish with details that paint purposefully.

Now stand back and see!

Iris Carignan

Surprising Terrain

Sometimes the pathway of an artist can be difficult, filled mostly with rocks, holes, pitfalls and dust. Yet, no matter, we continue down our personal pathway with passion and determination. Whether or not one is an artist, the pathway presented to each of us will at times be hard to deal with. In Romans 5 we learn of the importance of perseverance as we sojourn. The type of difficulty we encounter along the route of life is sometimes the result of our own doing. Our own missteps can lead us into troubled pathways not intended for the believer. Romans 6:1-6 reminds us that "since we have died to sin" we should "walk in newness of life" and "we should no longer be slaves of sin."

Some of the rough terrain we encounter may be the practical kind. As artists, financial stones often trip us up. There is a long-standing reason why the label "starving artist" often applies and it shouldn't surprise us, but of course it does. While being an artist brings great blessing and joy with the creation experience, the lot of an artist also commonly includes meager and unstable earnings. Paul challenges us in Philippians to learn that "no matter what state" we are in, to "be content."

Artists are quite often more emotional in response to the challenges of life, or perhaps it is really that we are naturally more demonstrative. Our pathway may become muddy with emotional gloom. The very next day we may see life as clean, sure and bright with God's light directing our pathway in hope and clear direction.

Regardless of what the road may bring us, God's word reminds me "I can do all things through Christ who strengthens us" (Philippians 4:13).

Painting a Picture of Faith

As an artist and teacher, I have had the opportunity to help others learn how to paint. My favorite subject is landscapes, especially landscapes that include calm, reflective water. It occurred to me that the process of painting a landscape is a good metaphor for how we should approach our life as believers. The steps below are given when leading students through the process of painting a landscape. The text in italics are the spiritual metaphors for life's journey. Our God is the great Master Creator of the universe and of each person. All artists who strive to become better in their craft usually seek a teacher or master artist to help them learn to paint well. They listen and study the teacher's methods to put them into practice. Sometimes the paintings work out well, but regardless of success, any artist who truly wants to learn will keep painting. Through perseverance, artists and believers alike will begin to succeed as they "paint" their way through life. All believers who claim that Jesus is their Lord are stating that He is their master. When someone is your master, then you try your best to please him and to do all that he commands you to do. If He is your master by choice, you do everything out of love, not obligation or law.

These step-by-step instructions are meant as general guidelines for successful painting and living:

1. Start with the horizon line. Decide how much of the composition is the heavenly part and how much is below it. Have a plan; decide what is most important in the picture you want to paint. *This can also be applied to our spiritual lives and the picture of our life that we hope will be painted as we live it out. Do we see our time on earth as the most important and eternal thing, or is our eternal life more important in the grand scheme of things?*

2. Lay in the big shapes and general colors. *Decide what the big goals in life are and which ones are most important in shaping your life.*

3. Decide on the key focal point. *In the big picture of life, what one thing should stand out to others when they look at the picture of my life? What should be the most important thing to me?* What kinds of things will make it evident as the focal point? *Realize that in every picture there must be some dark colors and some light colors or it will be pretty dull. Remember that the contrast of the darkest color next to the lightest color draws attention to things, so use this to advantage whenever considering the focal point.*

4. Stand back and look at what you have so far. Look to see if the overall design is good. Make any changes needed before getting too committed to the wrong course. *Whatever stage of life we are at, it is always a good idea to step back and look at what we are doing. Examine from a godly perspective as to whether or not we are on the right course. Have we strayed off course in some way? We need to make any changes in our life before we are too committed and it's harder to change.*

5. Start at the top of the canvas, which is usually the sky area *(or heavenly realms)*. You want to layer your colors according to the best way the medium works, so if there are dark objects that overlap into the sky area, make sure when using oil paint that they are gently laid in before you put the light colors of the sky. It is better to paint around them than to paint a dark color on top of the light. Make sure you look closely at your reference photo. *We always need to go back to our heavenly goals. Starting with what matters to God will affect how we layer our*

lives effectively. Make sure your reference is God's word and you refer to it often throughout the process.

6. Lay in your darkest darks where you see them but do not use black. Don't make everything dark. Only make the darkest where it is most effective like next to the focal point. Remember there is no color without light and whatever light is on, will affect its color and brightness. *The dark days of life can reveal God's redemptive hand. He is shining light that overcomes the darkness. Do not let the blackness of evil creep into the picture of your life. It will make all the colors of your life get muddy easily. Remember that Jesus is the light of the world. The absence of Jesus' light will mean the absence of color and life.*

7. Start defining shapes of objects a little more. Lay in subtle color differences. Push some colors to give more interest and also to create the illusion of distance. Remember colors that are grayed down will recede and give the effect of being farther away. *In life, we constantly need to push away the less important things. We also need to put behind us the things of the past that hinder God's purpose for us. Use the negative shapes to help define and shape the positive and important things in life. Looking at the negative shapes often reveals the correct shapes, proportions and distance of other things.*

8. Step back again and look to see how it's going. Has the focal point faded in importance? Evaluate the progress. *Are you still taking the purpose of your life's picture where it should go? Is God still your focal point?*

9. Look more closely at your reference now. Do you see something you didn't notice before? Do you need to

correct or add anything? *Continue to read God's word. Has He revealed anything new to you that you need to change, or are you joyous with what He has shown you? Do you need to make any adjustments to your life's picture at this stage?*

10. Paint in more details, especially in the important things. Leave out some details where they aren't necessary. The things closest in the picture usually need more detail and attention. Let the painting direct you; if you feel a tug at the brush, go with it. Sometimes a painting will seem to have an energy or kind of "force" that tells you what to do. *Make sure you pay attention to the details of life that are most important. Too often we get so caught up with distractions in life that we ignore the best, including those who are closest to us. Let God's Spirit guide and direct how you paint each day. Let His hand take you where you need to go. His spirit is the only true "force" we can trust. He always knows the best course to take, and when we feel His spirit guiding, we need to let Him make the brushstrokes.*

11. Step back again and see how it looks. Is there anything more you need to do that will make it a better picture? *Take another look along life's way to see if you need to do anything better.*

12. Start putting in the final accents in color and light -- the jewelry or sparkle, the bling that makes it sing. Now's the time to put those things in, not at the beginning. Using just the right amount of punch at the end will make the difference in a beautiful painting, rather than a dull and cluttered one. *Let your light so shine before men, that they may see your good works and glorify your Father in heaven"* (Matthew 5:16)

13. Now sign it! You're done! You're done! (Yes, say it to yourself at least twice). Do you feel good about the work before your eyes? Make sure you aren't comparing your work to other artist's work when you evaluate its beauty. There will always be another artist who is better in some way. Be glad you have finished the painting. *Thank God for working His purposes together in your life to create a beautiful painting of His love. Think of all the times He added things, took things away, pulled things together, allowed darkness to show you His light and brought color in your life. Remember, without light there is no color. Do you see God's brushstrokes or did you try to control things too much? Will others see the main point in your life's picture? Make sure you aren't comparing your painting to other artist's work to evaluate. None of us are perfect artists, only the Almighty Creator of the universe is a perfect artist. Comparing ourselves to others is not a valid measure, for "All have sinned and fall short of the glory of God" (Romans 3:23). Only when we let God be the master artist, can we truly paint a beautiful and lasting picture (see 1 Corinthians 3:12-15).*

Creative Insights

The old adage, *Time flies when you're having fun,* is one that as an artist I can identify with. The act of creating a piece of art is one of the most pleasurable gifts God has graced me with. Indeed, time does seem to fly when I am in the midst of painting or some other artistic endeavor. I have often heard my art students say the same thing. Ironically, there is an actual neurological reason for that seemingly timeless void during the creation process.

Scientists believe that the right side of the brain is the artistic side and that the process of measuring time is not a function of that part. In other words, it is virtually impossible to use that cranial section to sense the passing of time. Thankfully, we can switch over to any part of the brain without having to push some button, stand in a different position, tilt our heads or shake vigorously, not most of us, anyway. We can also know that "Because of our faith, Christ has brought us into this place of undeserved privilege where we now stand, and we confidently and joyfully look forward to sharing God's glory" (Romans 5:2 NLT).

It was during one of my art class inspiration breaks that we began discussing the subject of time. I had just read a short devotion that spoke of the joy of being in the presence of God. It expounded on the promise that someday we believers will be with Him forever. The discussion then moved to the concept of eternal life. I brought up the insight that God had given me regarding Einstein's Theory of Relativity, as mentioned in "Time Theories." (See pages 73 and 74) In the middle of my explanation, God gave me another insight regarding time. It hit me that as artists, we have the special privilege of experiencing a slice of eternal existence every time we create because we are using the right side of the brain. When we are with the Lord and in His state of eternal existence, we will no longer be living in the restraints of time. Therefore, artists have a glimpse of the rapturous joy and fun promised in eternal life where time ceases. We see in 1 Peter 5:10 that "In His kindness God called you to share in His eternal glory by means of Christ Jesus."

God's Creative Gene

I have often felt that as artists, we have an extra dose of God's creative gene and therefore should be more tuned into His Spirit. Sadly, my experience in the art world has not always proven this. Like any other vocation, the field of art is permeated with various opinions, impressions and influences of the world it abides in. The varied definitions of art we encounter baffles the sense of clarity as to what it truly is, so why should we be surprised.

Several years ago I met an artist who had frequently professed to be a Christian. However, the more I became acquainted with him, the more doubt I had of his faith. One evening he called and asked me if I would invite his wife to my church. Of course I was happy to do so, but hadn't had the opportunity to get acquainted, so felt awkward doing so. After suggesting that he also attend with us, I was informed that he "didn't need church." Having observed in past months that he had a drinking problem, it was incongruent with his witness. I decided to talk with him at the following art guild meeting and again encourage his church attendance as well. Because his claim of being "a Christian" was murky at best, I decided to find some common spiritual ground to build on.

After several attempts to establish some shared beliefs, I found myself at the most basic question I could think of. I said "You believe in God, don't you?"

To which he replied: "No!"

My mouth must have dropped wide open at this surprising response. "I don't understand," I said "Why do you call yourself a Christian if you don't even believe in God?"

"Well," he went on, "doesn't being Christian mean you do nice things for other people?"

Needless to say, my quest for finding common spiritual ground jolted to an abrupt stop.

God's word encourages us to "sow the seed" of the gospel to those we meet along our path, and I did my best to do that with this person. However, I never did see any evidence of spiritual awakening in him after that day.

Muddy Paths

Any artist who paints knows that there is one color you never want to put in your painting, and that is *mud*. Now this isn't a color you can buy in a tube or jar, and it is really a non-color. But what has been dubbed as "mud" is the result of many wrong colors mixed together.

With life, we see that the temptation to mix a little lie with the truth can lead to trouble and also muddy-up our life. We read in Genesis 3:13 of how Satan tempted Eve to eat of the forbidden fruit. If you read it carefully, you'll see that much of what he said to her was the truth. He just mixed in a little lie or two, and colored the truth with distortions. These lies mixed with the beauty of the fruit were just enough to convince Eve to sin. Jesus referred to Satan as the "father of lies" (John 8:44) and says that telling lies is consistent with who he is and always has been.

We continue to see evidence of the evil one's influence in our society today. Unfortunately, too many Christians don't know the truth well enough to spot a lie. We may be so impressed with the beautiful color that has been painted that we buy into the lie.

In Psalm 7:14 it says, "The wicked conceive evil; they are pregnant with trouble and give birth to lies. They dig a deep pit to trap others, then fall into it themselves". One of the most frequently used methods of deception is repetition of a mistruth. Many businesses and organizations whose motives are less than honorable have used this technique effectively to influence large segments of our society. They have discovered that if they tell a lie often enough, loud enough and to enough people, it will be believed.

How can we best sort through all the information that bombards our minds and souls every day? Is there any way we can discover the truth about important moral, ethical and spiritual issues? For centuries, the Bible has been the one consistent source of truth that has withstood time, as well as societal and cultural changes. In it we read that we can ask God to give us the gift of discernment to distinguish the truth from a lie. We also read that the author and finisher of our faith in God's truth never changes, for it says: "Jesus Christ is the same yesterday and today and forever" (Hebrews 13:8).

Surprising Soil

We are told in Matthew, Mark and Luke that when we sow the seed of God's Word, we will be casting it onto four kinds of soil: good soil, bad soil, thorny soil, and rocky soil. It has long been my heart's desire to bring many into the kingdom of Christ. However, while I have often worked, prayed and tried to bring others to the Lord, most often I do not see the fruits of my labor. It is frustrating and heartbreaking to have a loved one forsake faith. I remind myself that it's His Holy Spirit who draws someone into faith, not me. My job is to plant and water along the way.

In the art classes that I teach, my students all know and expect me to give an inspirational thought during our break. During one such break, the prophetic accuracy of God's "Farmer's Almanac," otherwise known as the Bible, revealed itself. Just two weeks before, I had given one of my usual short devotionals of inspiration as we sat together relaxing and eating a snack. That particular thought for the day had led to some interesting discussion and commentary.

It had shocked and surprised me to hear some of the errant comments from a few of my students regarding core issues of faith. Their comments regarding salvation did not even align with their own religious denominations. Two weeks later and after a lot of prayer and consideration, I felt compelled to give them a more direct word addressing these questions and comments. I chose to read directly from the Bible instead of my usual small booklet of devotions. One of the passages I read that morning was John 14:6: "I am the way, the truth and the life, no one comes to the Father except through me." It was my intention that day to give them God's word directly and not my own thoughts or the thoughts of some other book. As one would expect, there were some who didn't take it well. One of them was a gentleman who was from a mixed religious background and had often said that he was spiritually open and frequently read the Bible. In his anger, he stormed out of the room and called later to say he was dropping my class. Another was a woman student relatively new to the class.

In our walk, we know that there will be many along the way who will not respond to God's word positively. While I was disappointed with their reaction, God gave me great peace in my spirit about it all. Interestingly, five months later, it occurred to me how prophetically suitable the woman's negative reaction was. She had called me that night to say how offended she was and that she too was dropping out of my art class. In my attempt to explain that I had felt God leading me to read His word, she rudely hung up on me. For months afterwards I found myself thinking about her occasionally, but couldn't seem to remember her name. Then, during a Bible study that talked about the four kinds of soil, the irony suddenly hit me because her name was *Rocky.*

Painted Colors of the Sky

Did you touch a leaf today?
Or see the plants that grow?
Have you felt the warmth of sun
Or know the ways of a crow?

And has the fragrance of a rose
Convinced your heart
Not just your nose,
Of how it all happened
And who made all of those?

Have you listened to the robin sing
A song that lifts your spirit?
Just be still a moment and maybe
You will hear it.

Painted colors of the sky
Are the artwork of our
God on high.
And were they framed as paintings
In our hearts,
They'd be of more value than any fine art.

The clock ticks,
The drum rolls,
The clanging bell
For whom it tolls
Life's metronome within us stored
By our composer
Is a grand symphony score

"The grass withers,
the flower fades"
And so also our bodies to the grave.

And someday it's clear we all will see
Our creator and maker
And before Him we'll be.

Iris Carignan, 2011

67

Chapter 5

Leading In His Time

His Amazing Answers to Prayer

They say that hindsight is always 20/20 and it's so true. I've often teasingly asked my optometrist if he could give me better hindsight. Reading through old journal entries can also bring good hindsight into our contemporary life. The following story is an entry from my journal as written seventeen years ago. Its date of entry indicates that there had been an eleven-year gap between entries.

> *Dear Journal,*
>
> *Well, it's been a long time old pal, but here I am again. So much has happened since my last entry, no doubt I could fill this book. But for now, I just want to say how I came back to this journal. The Lord has been telling me for several months, through Bible studies (led by Larry and me), to write in my journal, but I kept forgetting or putting it off.*
>
> *Last night while saying bedtime prayers, I felt especially led to start journaling again and feared that*

by morning I would forget. So I prayed that God would remind me to find this journal and begin making entries again.

The next morning I sat down and picked up my devotional guide (15 Minutes Alone With God by Emilie Barnes) and read: "Thoughts for action: <u>Write down in your journal</u> several blessings or incidents of God working in your life."

So there was my reminder. And here I am again.

Documenting all of our trials, worries, prayers and praises is one of the best faith builders we could do for ourselves. The Bible itself is filled with hundreds of recorded accounts of God's children in their journey. We have the advantage of reading all of them today and learning from them. Journaling is one of the best markers of faith that a believer can give himself. If you haven't started one yet, do so today. If you are worried that you will not have time to write every day, don't fret. So, if you want to improve faith's hindsight, get busy writing your journal, then be sure to read it once in awhile. Who knows whether someone may someday benefit from your recorded words as well.

The Valley of the Shadow

My father passed away in 1996 and for more than a year, I did not enter anything into my journal. Losing a parent is one of the most devastating losses we can experience and we don't realize just how impacting it will be until it happens.

My dad was a good father who always did his best to provide. We did not live luxuriously in material things, but our lives were rich with his creative imagination and adventurous spirit. He was born in Chicago, Illinois. The rest of us were born in Georgia, and for the first five years of my life, we lived in the South. My father had always loved baseball and just months before WWII broke out, he was invited by the minor league division of the Cubs to try out. Unfortunately, the war destroyed his chances to play professional baseball. After the war and a few attempts at other vocations, he settled on sign painting. His artistic eye and ambidextrous hands lent themselves well to this endeavor. When work grew scarce in Georgia, we moved to Florida. After spending about a year there with little improvement, my family moved to California.

For the rest of his working days, Dad worked hard to make his sign business successful, but jobs came sporadically. One of his favorite pick-me-up sayings was: *"When my ship comes in, we'll..."* A lot of those years he used our detached garage as his sign shop. I will always remember the times I would wander into his shop and ask if I could paint something too. He would give me some paper, paint and brushes and set me up on a stool. So, I would paint a picture while he would paint a sign next to me. It's a Norman Rockwell kind of picture that is painted into my memory. I am sure that those special early moments did much to shape my interest in art.

Dad was rarely short on good humor with plenty of jokes and puns to lift our spirits. Some of those jokes grew a bit stale after the hundredth time or two and he knew it. They became his standards for rubbing in a little "old fun" and got more laughs at our rolling eyes than the worn out humor. Dad had other talents too that never got the acclaim or polish they deserved. One of them was his beautiful voice. It was a tenor voice like

Frank Sinatra's and he loved to sing as he drove us on a trip to the store or on vacation. We didn't take a lot of vacations in my youth, but his favorite thing seemed to be camping and fishing. My brothers and I loved the great outdoors, too, and always thought of those times as adventures. When Dad just felt like getting away for a while but couldn't really take a vacation, he would say, "Let's go for a drive!" Off we'd go for hours, usually looking for a "ghost town" as he called them. We didn't find many ghost towns, but the exciting anticipation of it all was enough for the day's journey.

Sadly, Dad's last months and days were difficult as he battled many health issues, including kidney failure. Ironically, the week he passed away, my mother received an official letter stating that she had inherited some money from a distant uncle. I tried desperately to encourage healing for my dad in his last days by telling him "his ship had come in, for real this time." My dad had served in the Navy during the war and now God had sent another kind of ship, one that brought some assurance for my mother's well being, and another to take him home to rest. I wonder if he continues painting signs up in heaven for the Lord. If so, perhaps they occasionally make it down here and guide me on my journey until we are reunited eternally.

"Yea, though I walk through the valley of the shadow of death, I will fear no evil" (Psalm 23:4).

A Lesson Well Lived

Life is a lesson both lived and taught,
By all who enter with an open heart.
It catches our attention
Mostly in the rough
And slides by quickly
With all the easy stuff.

Some come through it with ease
And little strain,
While others, like diamonds, are
Refined by much pain.

The sparkle of their love to all who
Come close
Is the enduring jewel we treasure the most.

He taught me to laugh and to love, and to live.
My father always had so much to give.

His riches, not earthly, are banked
In my heart.
Praise God, this kind never departs.

And following him to heaven
These treasures he built
By God's promise
Won't rust, wither or wilt.

Then again there's the jokes he did tell
Not the funny ones
But the ones that grew stale.

I thought: If God allowed them in heaven
With its eternal existence,
Their endless repetition,
Might be to heaven's host
A hellish perdition.

But I'm guessing when Jesus did meet him at the gate,
Like the sins he was cleansed of, they too
Did flake!

There's another part of Dad that he passed on to me,
It's the love of painting and
Artistic creativity.

As a child by his side he let me stand
Dad painting signs
Me painting pictures, brushes in our hands.

And now this child of God
Up in heaven's sign shop,
Stands next to the master
Painting on without stop.

Iris Carignan, 1996

Time Theories

As believers, we quickly learn that our hopes, prayers and
questions don't always get answered in the time or way we think

they should. Ancient history and God's story as told in the Bible is full of examples of how man strives to control his environment and his god. One common human struggle is our constant fight against time. There just doesn't seem to be enough of it for most of us. Since my youth, I have often pondered questions of how some aspects of science and nature may actually be reinforced by God's word and vice-versa. While studying in a college astronomy class years ago, I was blessed with an epiphany of wisdom that could have only come from God, certainly not my pocket-sized brain. It was regarding Albert Einstein's Special Theory of Relativity presented around 1915.

In simple terms, Einstein's theory says, in part, that an observer will note a slowing of clocks and time, and shortening of rulers if they are moving with a speed near the speed of light. This part of the theory is also known as "time dilation." He was saying, in so many words, that all forms of measurement, including time, are affected as they near the speed of light. While studying this during my college years, it suddenly hit me that this scientific theory is compatible with the concept of eternal life and God's eternal existence. I surmised that if we consider the word of God which describes God the Father and Jesus as being "light" or the "light of the world" (John 8:12), we could apply God's word to the scientific theory regarding time. Spiritually, we could say that as we approach, or come near God, who is light, we too will see time slow down and ultimately stop, become nonexistent or *eternal.*

As that morsel of enlightenment struck me, I could barely contain my excitement. The next day of my astronomy class, I had the opportunity to ask my professor about my application of Einstein's theory. He seemed both surprised and impressed at this concept and even confirmed that it made sense to him as well. It was a rare intellectual experience for my limited brain and knowledge, but my Lord continues to amaze me as I seek to know Him better.

The Englishman Sir William Russell must have caught a glimpse of this truth as well back in 1683, when he took out his pocket watch just as he was about to meet his death on the scaffolds. He gave it to the doctor attending him and said "Would you take it, for I have no use for it. I am dealing with eternity now." When we fully enter eternity through the death of our earthly bodies, we will no longer be under the restraints of time.

We will be eternally next to Him in His heavenly realm, and time will not exist with us anymore, just as it never did with Him. Our mighty God is the great "I Am." He is and was and always will be in existence.

As I reflect on the many times in my life when the unexpected and undesired happened, it has become clearer that I am not in charge. Quite a revelation, huh? As humans, I think that control and man's finiteness may be the two most difficult realities we struggle with. When God created the heavens and the earth, He set in motion the constraints of time that all humans deal with. Albert Einstein is quoted as saying: *The distinction between the past, present and future is only a stubbornly persistent illusion.*

In His infinite love, God gave humanity the exclusive gift of free will and the intelligence to use time in a fruitful way. Whatever level of intelligence one may have, none of us have the all-knowing, prophetic, and eternal perspective that our Creator has. He alone sees the past, present and future all at once, for God is not confined to a table of time. Praise God!

Einstein Saw The Light

Though a father of science
This great mind was he
Einstein would admit
Oh so humbly,
That next to his creator,
Even brilliant insight
Could not measure up
Because Einstein saw the light!

In respect to measured dimensions of life,
We tend to measure good deeds vs. bad
Happiness vs. strife
We hope to pack them in our bags (or unpack as it
may be)
Before making that final flight
Into His immeasurable eternity,
And into His eternal light.

Iris Carignan 1984

Cute Shoes—Beautiful Feet

While getting my hair done at my favorite beauty salon, both
my hairdresser and I overheard the aesthetician talking to her
client about some beautiful sandals she'd seen at a boutique.
"They were really beautiful," she said. "They had these beautiful

blue rhinestones on them," she repeated with elaboration. "So," she went on, "I asked how much they cost. Would you believe, they were $3,900.00? Well, that was just a little too high for me," she concluded.

"At that price," I told my hairdresser, "those shoes ought to take you places too."

The lady went on and on about these sandals, repeatedly mentioning how beautiful they were. Unable to avoid eavesdropping, both my hairdresser and I couldn't help but smile as we considered the obvious temptation she was apparently struggling with regarding those outrageously priced sandals. As if in response to her embellishments about the beauty of the sandals, God whispered this verse to me: "How beautiful are the feet of those who bring good news" (Romans 10:15 NIV).

It just so happens, like many women, I too love shoes. For me, the right pair of shoes can make or break the look of any outfit. Sadly, my aging arthritic toes are no longer able to wear some of the most stylish and beautiful shoes I own, so they adorn my closet now. Recently a friend told me that her husband appreciates shoes as well, but insists that every pair of shoes in their closet have a shoetree to keep their proper shape. Immediately I went to the humor of it: *If I had to put a shoetree in every pair of shoes in my closet, they might have to cut a whole forest down to accommodate them.*

The more I contemplated the verse that continued to roam my thoughts, the more I saw the connection to my deeper desire to bring the good news of salvation to others. Could it be that the Lord is trying to adorn my feet in a new way, and that He wants to take my feet to new places?

I pray my journey and yours will indeed take us to new places—places where only the Lord can adorn our feet with beauty. This beauty is costly, but no worries—He has already paid it in full.

Stepping Out of the Boat

I recently joined a different Bible study. It was a small step, yet an unsteady, uncertain step. After more than twenty-five years in the same study group, the niggling urge for fresh growth that had vexed my spirit for more than two years finally found courage. Mind you, I wouldn't compare this baby step to Peter's stepping out of the boat to walk on water. However, after several weeks of prayer and seeking God's direction, I finally made the change and "walked on water" (Matthew 14:22-31). I knew that I must follow my Lord's leading, even if former group members would be hurt. He was calling me out of the boat that hindered my spiritual growth. He was calling me to focus on Him, not the people in the boat.

The summer before this brave move, I had tested the waters at a seven week Beth Moore Bible study. The format, the in-depth study and the mixture of both young and mature faces that joined together in search of spiritual growth was a breath of fresh air blowing into my soul. It was exactly what I needed to shake out my doldrums—a group of women of all ages, a compelling study that drove me once again into God's word, and an opportunity to mentor younger women.

After tasting the joy of that summer group, I was eager to find a new study group to join. Our large church had a variety of women's Bible study groups, but I sought God's leading to the one He had for me. It wasn't as if Jesus stood at the end of the hall, saying: *Come to this one.* After prayer and some trepidation, I chose another Beth Moore study. But after two weeks, I knew that I'd chosen incorrectly. Should I climb back into the safety of my prior boat or try another one I'd considered?

As I walked up to the leader to explain why this study wasn't suited for me, I encountered another woman who felt the same. We struck up a conversation as we left the room and had lunch together. I made a new friend who wanted to join our evening home Bible study. The Lord had this encounter in mind when I attended the wrong study group after all. No wonder I felt conflicted, but away I went with a new confidence of walking on the water of His calling.

As I settled into the new study group, each week my Lord reaffirmed His leading. Shortly after starting, He reached out His hand with an unexpected reward for making this move— the honor of serving through singing. The worship leader is the same sister who led worship in the summer study and who asked if I would like to assist in leading the praise and worship. It has been about ten years since I've had that privilege and I've missed it dearly. My Lord knows the desires of our hearts and prepares us to receive them in due time. Isaiah 55:11–12 says "You shall go out with joy..." Oh, the joy when we climb out of our safe boats, fix our eyes on Him and walk where He leads.

Winds of Time

Time rushes by like the wind upon the ocean.
Pushing petulant white caps regardless of my notions.

Treasured moments I would still and hold
Whip past me like a fury,
Never to blow my way again.
Oh Lord, what's the hurry?

Time was once a soft whispered breeze,
Gentle and warm and doing as I please,
But the winds of childhood grew steady and fast
Once beyond youth's shortened grasp
And storms at times blew harder than now,
But settled quickly to a peaceful blow.

Time's wind is now steady and strong against my face
Not slowing yet this runner nears the end of her race

Oh to catch time in my soul
And rest it on a bench.
Seated with my loved ones,
This heart's thirst 't would quench

But the evening breeze whistles a song
Through death's narrow tunnel
Its' melody lifts my spirit
Sifting the winds of time
With God's gracious funnel.

For time, says the song, is but a man-made wind
That's blown away at life's end
And harnessed by angel's wings.
The winds of eternal life
Forever softly sing.

Iris Carignan

Chapter 6

Surprising Connections

Rainbow's Reach

Like a rainbow arching from here to there
Love's transparent color reaches
from me to you,
When God's light is shining through.

Iris Carignan, 2003

Wheels of Contentment

"Would you pray for me, Joni?" That was the plea my friend, Doug Mazza, gave to his friend, Joni Eareckson Tada, as he entered his office to pick up a few things he needed for a speaking engagement. Doug is the president of Joni and Friends, a worldwide disability ministry and was on his way to a conference to speak on their behalf. He has a lot of experience with speaking engagements, but for some reason he was feeling uneasy about this particular one. Deep down, he knew it stemmed from concern over his son's upcoming surgery. It was scheduled for the day after this three day Disability Awareness conference. The time constraints of the long drive from L.A. to Fresno, California and back were weighing on his heart. To his surprise, Joni didn't pray that he would feel good or confident about this conference. No, she prayed that God would show him the reason he was being sent to Fresno.

Doug had already come a long way from his earlier days as an executive and COO of Hyundai Motors. The detour directing him to a new road in life was the knee-buckling experience of having a child born with severe disabilities. Ryan was his third child and the doctors had no idea that anything was wrong until his birth. Since that day, there had been dozens of surgeries and many anxious moments. Yet, through the years of dealing with such unexpected and devastating difficulties, Doug had learned much about God. The chaos of dealing with everything had taught him the difference between joy and contentment.

He had learned that contentment is knowing that he is where God wants him to be. He cried out to God to show him Ryan's purpose in life, and through all of the tribulations with his son, God showed him his own purpose. At that point in time, one small verse in Psalm 116:1b rose to the top of his heart: "He hears my voice and my prayer for mercy." So while Doug went away feeling some comfort after Joni's prayer that day, he would tell you honestly that he still wasn't feeling particularly excited about going the distance to Fresno.

The last of the five speaking appointments that weekend had finally come. Doug was hoping there wouldn't be the same throng of people coming to him after this last talk so he could get on the road quickly. But, alas, after wrapping it up, several people began making their way down the aisle to talk and pray with him. He watched as one wheelchair-bound woman was quickly passed by, placing her last. "My name is Diana," she began. "I want to tell you my life's story." Though cringing with quiet apprehension at the prospect of a lengthy delay, Doug listened patiently. Diana went on to say she was born with Cerebral Palsy and grew up in a small town in New Jersey. She had struggled all her life to have even the simplest and most normal kinds of things, including an education. Although she was bright, authorities had placed her in a school for mentally disabled children. Her father had been her biggest advocate and was finally able to convince the public school to allow her enrollment in eighth grade. She was the first person in a wheelchair to ever enter this three-level public school, but it had no elevator. The principal called her into his office on the first day of school and introduced her to a senior student on the football team. "This boy," he said, "is going to make sure you get up the steps and to all your classes."

Diana went on to say that as each class ended, seeing her senior friend waiting outside the classroom door to help was a great comfort to her. "In fact," she confessed, "I had a crush on him because he was so faithful." Not having any friends made things pretty tough, but, with the support of her father and the help of others, she had graduated and gone on to become an attorney.

Doug stood in shocked realization as he carefully studied Diana's face and mentally peeled away forty years of time. "Did you say you were born in New Jersey?" He asked.

"Yes!"

"Diana," Doug declared, *"I was that football player!"* Her face lit up in surprised elation as reality sank in. His wife, Lorraine, joined them as Diana's wheelchair bounced in uncontained joy and they all praised God together.

God had indeed revealed the reason why Doug needed to be there. He often says that "God gives us the first step, then we watch what He does." He had taken many first steps in life; some, he learned, included that first encounter with a wheelchair long ago in high school. God had taken Doug on a circuitous route from New Jersey to the wheels of the auto industry, then the wheelchair of his own son, to Wheels for the World at Joni and Friends and back around to that blessed moment in Fresno, California. The full realization that from early on, God had His hand on Doug's life came into focus like never before. Once more, he was content knowing that he was right where God wanted him to be, and he was joyful, too. "For I know the plans I have for you, says the Lord, They are plans for good and not for disaster, to give you a future and a hope. In those days when you pray, I will listen" (Jeremiah 29:11–12 NKJ).

Surprising and Serendipitous Connections

Throughout the New Testament, fellow believers are referred to as friends and as brothers and sisters in Christ, especially by the apostle Paul. Over the years, we have recurrently experienced this amazing spiritual connection with the family of God. Several years ago, my husband and I took an exciting cruise to Europe. While on this large vessel that carried a few thousand people, we found ourselves bumping into one particular couple over and over. They both seemed like nice, fun-loving people and eventually we introduced ourselves to one another. To our surprise, we learned they lived about twenty minutes from our home in California. They not only lived nearby, Scott and Twila were fellow believers and knew many of the same people we knew. They also attended the same church our oldest son attended. We instantly became friends as we realized our commonalities.

In the years since that serendipitous meeting, we have continued to socialize with these two special people and through them our circle of friends has grown even bigger. Even more amazingly, just last year these two friends had another fantastic "chance meeting." While checking my e-mail one afternoon, my mouth dropped wide open as I read the note from my friend and art student, Stacy. She was on a cruise in Europe and had just met her assigned tablemates. They had all introduced themselves and learned the domicile of each person as well as their interests. When Stacy mentioned she was from our area in California, one of the couples asked if she knew us.

"Know them!" she exclaimed with great astonishment, "I take art classes from Iris."

The couple happened to be Scott and Twila, our friends yet unknown to Stacy, until that moment. Thus another sisterly connection and friendship was made while across the ocean in Europe.

Chapter 7

Wounded and Thirsty Hearts

When Thirsty Hearts Be Quenched

The flowers lift their heads
With mouth and heart wide open
Receiving from the heavens
His grace in rain that's given.

With praises lifted in response
We see their leaves are raised
In thanks to Him who gave them life
And considered all their days.

Oh that we would praise as well
When thirsty hearts be quenched
Would ne'r forget to lift our hearts
Nor cease to be content.

Iris Carignan, 2014

Thirsty Traveler

Here in Southern California we've had a terrible drought for the past couple of years, while most of the rest of the nation has been experiencing the worst winters in a hundred years. Yesterday the soft patter of rain blessed our land with a short-lived, partial quenching. The welcome refreshment mostly wet our tongues and left us like unrequited lovers, yearning for more. Oh, that we would also be as thirsty for our Lord.

The psalmist speaks to this in Psalm 42 as he describes his own desire for God. "As the deer pants for the water brooks, so pants my soul for You, O God. My soul thirsts for God, for the living God." Matthew 5:6 also reminds us that we should "hunger and thirst after righteousness." It goes on later in chapter 5 verse 13 to say: "You are the salt of the earth, but if the salt loses its flavor, how shall it be seasoned?"

How do these passages relate? Have you noticed that when you eat something salty, you always crave something to drink? I've noticed that pizza is a great thirst stimulator because of the high sodium content, creating thirst for hours after consuming a couple of slices. Thus, we can create a stronger thirst for our Lord by staying *salty*. Just for fun, I like to call it *pizza partnering*.

All of the beatitudes in Matthew 5 list the basic experiences and attitudes that we as Christians should be familiar with. They all begin with the word: "Blessed," showing us that our Lord knows the trials and emotions that plague us, yet He will bless us through them. They are a part of life, if we are truly salted believers. "You are the salt of the earth" is prefaced by the statement that we are "Blessed" when we are "reviled and persecuted falsely for His sake".

This tells me that while I don't strive for persecution, trials, and troubles, my attitude when they come should be one of joy and the effect should be a stronger thirst for my Lord. I pray that in my everyday encounters with others, my speech and actions will always be full of grace as well as salt, so that others will desire to know my savior. Perhaps my saltiness, sliced carefully with grace, will make me a better *pizza partner* as well.

Stacy's Story of Surprising Seeds

My friend, Stacy, is a unique and wonderful example of God's hand reaching down and grasping hold of a wanting spirit. She is a walking testimony to the impact of the smallest seeds of hope that land on fertile soil, to be watered and spring forth into new life. From the time she was a young girl, Stacy longed to know God, yet her family hadn't provided the kind of spiritual foundation that leads to a loving and personal relationship with God. Both parents were secular in their world view, devoid of spiritual inclination. Their lack of emotional connectedness should have nailed her inquisitive spirit to a religious coffin. Yet, throughout her youth, there were glistening jewels of spiritual truth that caught the eye of her heart.

When Stacy was a child, God planted seeds of hope in her heart through traditional Christmas music. The lyrics of "Oh Come All Ye Faithful," "Silent Night," and "Oh Little Town of Bethlehem" brought the true message of Christmas to the listening ears of a young girl's wanting soul. She began to perceive that there was more to Christmas than gifts and decorations.

Although Stacy and her younger brother grew up in the affluent community of Pacific Palisades, California, the distorted, dysfunctional diorama she lived in continually warped and obstructed the beautiful view of the ocean just beyond their house. Her father's detached and verbally abusive nature, paired with her mother's unrealistic idealization of life left her fending for herself. When troubles and worries weighed on her young soul, her mother was unapproachable for guidance and her father was aloof and rejecting. The more her mother ranted in fantasy about how perfect life was, the more bewildered she became.

As Stacy grew into her teens, she became increasingly depressed. Her search for spiritual direction took her to the study of world religions. After examining them, she concluded they couldn't all be right because there were too many contradictions between them. She then turned to the great philosophers like Plato and Socrates, but found no answers to the meaning or purpose of life through their writings.

As Stacy entered her twenties, she suffered frequent bouts of depression and discouragement that continued to dog her spirit. She slipped further into a spiritual vacuum, until her quest for purpose and truth brought her into a bookstore where another seed was planted in her soul. She spotted a book entitled "I Believe in Miracles." Her hungry soul devoured the many documented stories about everyday people who had experienced miracles. Story after story told of people healed of serious illness by their faith in Jesus. At that point she began to believe that God truly could help and heal people. A spark of hope became an ember in her soul that would later be fueled with the kindling word of God and the fire of His Holy Spirit. Yet she didn't fully know the saving grace of Jesus.

Stacy continued to wander through life like a lost sheep until one more piece of God's puzzle fell into place. She'd become independent of her parents and moved into an apartment during the 1960's, when downtown Hollywood was a fairly safe environment. However, the not so safe atmosphere of bars and nightclubs became her place of refuge. One night, as she walked aimlessly down the crowded yet lonely streets of her West Hollywood neighborhood, tears of hopelessness began streaming down her cheeks. That is when God gave her a clear sign, literally, painted on the side of a parked van. It read: "There is power in the blood of the Lamb." Immediately she felt drawn to the message and knew without a doubt that the answer to her search was somewhere within those words.

For several days she searched for the owner of the van in hopes of finding complete understanding of the message, only to realize that it was likely a disabled and abandoned vehicle. One night, while walking in a different area several miles from home, some people approached her and handed her a gospel tract. They asked Stacy if she knew Jesus Christ as her personal Lord and Savior. A conversation ensued, followed by unexpected joy and surprise as she learned they were the owners of the broken down van.

"I have been looking for you," she exclaimed with joy and relief. They invited her to a church service the following evening. She could hardly wait for work to be over and the church service to begin. Entering the church punctually at 8 p.m. that night, she immediately sensed the power of the Holy Spirit. Gospel songs filled the air with an exciting fervor like she had never heard before. Several people began to stand and give testimonies of how God had miraculously changed their lives from sin and the power of darkness to the power of light and hope. By the end of the service, God poured the water of His Holy Spirit on all the seeds previously planted in Stacy's heart. She moved toward the altar without hesitation and with a newfound purpose. She knelt down and received Jesus as her Savior. Stacy felt the filling of the

Holy Spirit and was born again at that moment. She was flooded with peace and joy "beyond all understanding."

Today Stacy continues to walk with the Lord and studies His Word in earnest. She no longer frequents bars and nightclubs, but there was a brief time of falling away. It happened when her husband of seventeen years suddenly left her for another woman, which cut a deep and painful trench that took a long time to climb out of. Yet God's persistent, loving hand reached out to her again and brought her back to His bosom. Now Stacy sows the seeds of God's love in all those whom she encounters along her purposeful journey. "Yet I will rejoice in the Lord, I will be joyful in God my Savior. The Sovereign Lord is my strength; he makes my feet like the feet of a deer, he enables me to go on the heights" (Habakkuk 3:17–19 NIV).

Sara's Story of Love and Visions

I'd like to introduce you to my friend Sara. You will love her because she herself is a loving person who exudes the love of Jesus, but if you knew her story, you might wonder how and why.

Let me begin by telling you that Sara was born into a Muslim family in Iran. Although her family did not practice the religion of Islam, everyone noticed that Sara seemed interested in spiritual matters from a very young age.

As a young woman, she fell in love and married an intelligent and handsome young man named Paul. About one year later, she gave birth to her first child and they were overjoyed with this blessing. However, it wasn't long before Sara realized that her husband struggled with depression and terrible mood swings, a hardship made worse by the fact that he refused to seek medical help. Although Paul clearly loved her and she loved him, Sara endured a long and difficult relationship fraught with harsh verbal abuse and numerous threats of suicide. Yet her love for him never failed.

In the late 70's, a revolution in Iran put new stress on their family and they sensed an urgent need to flee the growing hatred for Americans they were witnessing. So, they applied for a work visa to come to the U. S. When they were able to come, it was hard to find work and they didn't speak English well. Immigrants who come here legally do not receive any financial or medical aid and that made it especially difficult for their family too. They managed to find work at restaurants and other minimum wage jobs. Then they ran into an old friend from Iran who was able to get her husband a good job. Things began to turn around for them and four years after they arrived in America, Sara gave birth to their second child.

After several more years of financial struggles, they decided to move across country to California, but winding down on his job prevented Paul from moving at the same time as his family. So, with two young children in tow, Sara journeyed to another new land, but this time without the aid of her husband. Being alone with two young children in a new place became another hill for her to climb, but this was God's opportunity to respond to her seeking heart.

As she faced this separation from her husband, the walls of cultural differences closed in on Sara's spirit. A deep sense of loneliness began to cling to her soul. One day while walking her dog, she felt a strong tug on the leash. Her canine friend continued to pull her towards a woman who was also walking a dog. She had seen the lady a few times before but hadn't had the opportunity to meet her. She decided to take his lead and crossed the street to meet the lady. Surprisingly, that meeting would literally become a significant crossroad in her spiritual life.

To her delight, the woman was very friendly. They chatted for a long while and exchanged phone numbers. She learned that the woman was a Christian. That same week, her new friend called Sara and invited her to go to a Bible study that was just getting started. She considered the invitation for about a week, then Sara decided to give it a try; after all, she *was* lonely.

At the study each week, she found herself overwhelmed with emotion. She also joined a support group offered by the church for people who struggle with dysfunctional relationships. At that group, she met more new friends and gained new strength. More importantly, Sara began to learn more about the God of the Bible.

After a year, her husband was finally able to join her and the children in California. Being reunited with him was enjoyable at first, but quickly morphed back into the delicate balancing act of dealing with his psychological disorder. Added to this was the new realization that her son had his own emotional struggles. It was more than she thought she could bear, but it was only a small obstacle compared to trials that lay ahead.

Sara continued to attend the church and one day, suddenly realized that she loved Jesus. A strong sense of peace filled her as never before and she shared this with her new walking buddy. Eventually she told her husband, but he didn't say much, though he did notice a change in Sara. She had no idea how much her new faith would impact him and sustain her for the trouble ahead.

The first of an avalanche of trials that fell upon Sara and her family came when her son accidentally overdosed on his medication and passed away. This event devastated both Sara and her husband. His relationship with their son had always been detached and she saw that it hit him hard. Yet this tragedy became a pivotal point of spiritual vision for her. She began having extraordinary dreams and visions that would reaffirm and strengthen her new faith.

In the first dream, she was in a large church and heard someone say: "Jesus is coming, Jesus is coming." She saw Jesus, but couldn't see his face. Another dream came soon after, clearly expressing an attack of evil against God within her. But she ordered the devil to get away from her.

Two days after her son's passing, Sara was awake, sitting on her bed and crying in loud despair over her loss, sometimes screaming out in anguish and yelling at God. The pain in her heart felt like a heavy rock as she cried out to the Lord and asked: "Why, God? Why, why? I was a good mother, I loved him and he didn't do anything wrong. He didn't do anything wrong!" She suddenly saw a stunning, awesome vision. There before her eyes was Jesus, suffering and bleeding on the cross. He was saying, "It is finished," just as He spoke in John 19:30. During the vision, God the Father also said she should look at His son; because He didn't do anything wrong either. God gave her comfort by revealing that her own son's suffering is now finished too.

The vision's message couldn't have been any clearer. It sank deep into the hole in her heart and began its healing mission. She saw and felt the full power of God's love demonstrated to her. At that moment, Sara realized that God had also suffered the loss of his son, his perfect son. Even more, she sensed the mercy of what had happened to her own son, because he was suffering with mental illness and now would be whole and well.

Sara would have two more vivid dreams given to her after the vision. One was a dream that came the night after she asked God to let her see her son again. She did indeed see him clearly. In another dream she saw her son and heard him say that "he gave her one answer to the test, but she has to answer the other test herself."

That next test came in May of 2015. After forty-four years of marriage, the handsome yet troubled man she dearly loved took his own life. Added to the depression that had plagued Paul all his life was the more recent battle against cancer. It was more than he could handle.

While this terrible new tragedy in Sara's life could have broken her spirit completely, she has steadily found new strength and hope in the Lord. He gave her a vivid dream about her husband, too. In it she kissed him and told him that she loved him. Not long after her husband's passing, a family member encouraged her. She said that Sara had been the love that kept her husband going for so many years. Sara also recalled when her husband told her that he believed the same that she did about Jesus. He said he'd been watching her since she came to faith in Jesus. Sara found hope in that and believes that while her son and husband were detached in life, they are now united in love eternally.

Jesus continues to guide her through the storms and into the light of life. She now attends a large church as well as a few Bible studies. If you have the chance to meet her, you will see that despite the troubles she has been through, she continues to exemplify 1 Corinthians 13:13: "Now these three remain, faith, hope and love. But the greatest of these is love."

Unexpected Presence and Reassurance

Suzanne is a young woman who has come through the terrible pain of multiple miscarriages. With each one, the feeling of numbness and vulnerability grew. She continued to trust God and believe that His plan was perfect, yet the anguish was at times overwhelming. After two losses, she was pregnant again.

At twenty weeks, she began to relax and believe that it would hold, but sadly her hopes were dashed again. It was a baby girl and they decided to name her Julia. That was it! She could no longer hold back her anger at God. Her great anguish poured out in raging floods of tears and shouts at her Lord. Why was He doing this? Would she ever have a healthy baby? What becomes of these little ones that never have life outside the womb?

About a week after the devastating loss of the little baby girl, Suzanne and her husband were out working in the backyard when an unexpected feeling came over her. "It was an overwhelming sense of God's comfort and presence, like nothing I'd ever felt before. Even more, I sensed baby Julia was there too and she had been allowed to see her mother and father for a brief moment, perhaps as reassurance to me as well."

Suzanne did have another miscarriage that was at the same point of twenty weeks, and again she experienced God's overwhelming comfort and presence. Through all of this, she kept her faith and trust in God, and clung to the promise in Psalm 37 that God would "give her the desires of her heart." Finally, in 2012, she gave birth to a healthy little baby girl.

Suzanne and her husband would like to have another child, if God is willing. They continue to trust and know that He hears their prayers. Through all of their trials, they have become much stronger in their faith and know that whatever God does, His plan is perfect.

Behind His Throne—Victoria's Story

My friend Victoria is a beautiful child of God who has always demonstrated her faith in the Lord with love and grace. Our friendship began about forty years ago and has continued, even with her geographical distance the past twenty plus years. Despite our far-reaching friendship, it was only recently that I learned of a deep and painful experience she had. In His wisdom and timeliness, it was brought to my attention just as this collection of stories was nearing its completion.

Before I tell you the trial that my friend experienced, let me say that God revealed to her His mercy and His desire for this story to be shared. After many years of hiding her pain and guilt deep within her own soul, Victoria came to know that by sharing her mistake, pain and vision of hope, she can be a comfort and guide to other women.

Where are the children who were miscarried, aborted, or died very young? That is a question that many of us struggle with. We may be convinced that they are in heaven with God, yet many specific questions linger about what exactly that means. What are they doing there? Are they the same age as when they died? Who is taking care of them if they are still too young to do so? Where exactly do they exist in the heavenly realm? These questions, and many more, had continued to torment my friend Victoria as a result of a miscarriage that occurred early in her marriage.

It was in 1961, and just a year after her marriage, when she found herself pregnant with her first child. She was not thrilled with the idea of having a baby so early in her marriage because she didn't want to "divide time between a child and her husband."

Then, just a few months into the pregnancy, Victoria began having difficulties. She was having extreme morning sickness and began bleeding. Her doctor advised her to go home and stay off her feet, otherwise, he said, she would "lose the baby." The kind of job she had required her to be on her feet all day, so this was not going to be easy. However, because she was more concerned about dividing her time between her husband and baby, she ignored what the doctor said. "I didn't even tell my husband how serious it was, but continued to drag myself to work every day. Being a self-centered young woman, I only considered my desires and three weeks later, I got what I wanted—a miscarriage."

When it was all over, "I didn't ask if it was a boy or a girl." Victoria didn't care about the baby at that point. Her only concern was her relationship with her husband. Relief was all that she felt. "We went on with our lives and never looked back," she recalls.

Her secret sin lay dormant within her heart for many years before God brought the remembrance of the miscarriage and the child she lost. Strangely, the regret began sometime after her grandchildren were born. She was very excited to have grandchildren, yet feelings of guilt began to eat away at the blessing.

She began to have guilt and remorse for the baby that she believed she had "murdered" by neglect. The blessing of having two healthy grown children, and now having grandchildren, made her realize how precious each little soul is. Victoria felt she had broken the Lord's heart by not caring for that first little one.

A day came when she asked God's forgiveness. As she did, her heart seemed to crumble into pieces. "I was completely undone before the Lord. My tears would not stop." God's goodness and forgiveness comforted her during that time of healing and restoration. "He is so good," she testifies, "that He spoke into my spirit and told me that my baby was a little boy. Then He told me to give him a name."

Victoria named the little baby Thomas Clayton. "I felt overwhelmed with God's love and mercy towards me and thought: this is as good as it gets." Yet, even with this weighty release behind her, she didn't realize that God still had more to set before her.

One morning while she was praying, God gave her a vision of how glorious it is to be in His presence. "The vision touched me beyond anything my emotions can express. I couldn't write it down for the longest time because I would weep." As Vicki continued to tell of her overwhelming joy and awe at the vision she had experienced, tears brimmed her eyes again.

"I was transported into God's throne room," as it is described in Revelation 4:1–2 when John saw his vision. I saw that heaven was "vast and without walls. There were thousands of people; more than I could count. In my mind I heard them "praising the Lord and cheering me. I thought, why are these people so glad to see me? Then my Lord answered." She said He told her the people I saw were the people whom she touched for His sake and because she touched them, they touched others and gave testimony of God. He had comforted her with a glimpse of His glory and the fruits of her journey in life.

The vision continued as she found herself "walking down a long aisle and looking up at my King and Savior sitting on the throne. I could see that He was pleased to see me. Then I began to weep with joy." Victoria went on with the vision: "As I walked down the aisle, I felt a presence escorting me. I thought this must be my angel, but I could not take my eyes from my King to look. When I came close to Him, He reached out and wiped my tears away and drew me close. And we communed for a long time, yet did not use words."

Victoria continued with her amazing account. "Then I heard children laughing and singing." She was surprised to hear the happiness in their voices. "I looked and saw a little boy come running out from behind God's throne." She went on to describe the boy's brown eyes and hair color and his "plump" little body as typical of a child of about three years old. "He was dressed in a beautiful Asian style suit and wore a little hat on the back of his head, very much like a Jewish yarmulke. His eyes sparkled and I could hear his laughter as he ran towards me. At that moment I realized who this little boy was: he was the baby I miscarried— little Thomas Clayton. My tears flowed again and I was back in the present."

After this amazing experience, Victoria not only felt the great relief of forgiveness, she was filled with the joy of knowing her child was in God's inner sanctum and under the care of the ultimate father—the heavenly Father. She often finds herself replaying the image of the happy little children as they came out from behind God's throne. She not only realized God's forgiveness, but also sensed the forgiveness of all the children towards their parents. She said they all seemed to be waiting for "when their parents would come for them."

Victoria looks forward with complete confidence that one day she will see the child again and be allowed to raise him to adulthood in God's kingdom. What a glorious day it will be when my friend is able to call her child to come out from behind the Lord's throne for the rest of eternity.

Dancing In The Shadows

Are you dancing in the shadows,
Or are they dancing around you?

Can you feel their darkness?
And is it cool, or just blue?

When the warmth of sun
Is hot against your back,
And things seem oh so stark,
Is it hope or peace you lack?

And watching as you walk,
Do the shadows change?
Are they like a friend to you,
Or trouble dark and strange?

Shadows in the light will come
And so they too must be.
Shadows in my life have come,
And so also to thee.

Have you seen the way they dance,
When breezes blow both tree
And branch?
Their happy movement on the ground
With quiet music,
Yet sparkling sound.

But in the light of God's sweet love,
Life's shadows are short
When cast from above.

And in His light we have the chance,
To watch our troubles move
And even with them dance!

Iris Carignan, 2013

Morning's Dawn (No. 1 in a Trilogy)

Like the steel undergirding a bridge
And strengthening its long reach
Is the love of God upholding me.
Demonstrated, not just preached.

For He gave Himself
With truth spoken clearly
And to our grasping hands
His grip held tight
Across the span of darkness to love's pure light.

And as the truth does make its way
Into the wanting heart of one.
His glorious colors conquer the night
Breaking through in morning's dawn.

Iris Carignan, 2015

Chapter 8

A Journey Of Expectations

A Traveler's Notes

Our flight will leave soon and it will be a long one, yet only a portion of a three-legged trip. Larry and I are on our way to the U.K. and the very idea of seeing England, Scotland and Ireland ignites the romantic in me with visions of rolling, green hills and stone bridges over gentle streams. Startling me into reality, the flight attendant announces this flight will be eight hours long. My proclivity for metaphors pushes this interruption into the popular analogy of life being a "journey," with every blessing, trial, and phase as a leg in the overall ride. I think about how often we desire prophetic knowledge of how long each phase of the trip will be and to know the end of our days. If only God would send an angelic flight attendant to occasionally announce how long it will take to get through the rough stuff. But really now, would I change that much about my actions and behaviors? Would I tend to the most important things in life if I knew? I suspect not.

The plane hits some turbulence and we bump up and down a few times. Well of course, I go on philosophizing, life isn't just a journey, it's a roller coaster ride with lots of ups and downs, bumps and turns that never seem to get us anywhere. I wonder, is it any different for those of faith versus nonbelievers? I choose to believe that it is. One big difference being that at the end of a believer's ride is God's promised, eternal, heavenly destination and His welcoming arms upon our arrival. Faith in God and the Savior Jesus Christ may not stop the peaks and valleys of our human experience, but at the end of the ride we are home.

So why does it seem that during life's ride, God shows up at the least expected time? Just about the time things have leveled off, my anxious pleading stopped and the pounding of my fists no longer echo in the halls of "injustice," the unforeseen happens. Right in the middle of a mundane, or at best quiet phase, there He is. It also seems that most often it is during those peaceful times that He reveals His most astonishing and unexpected presence. Of course I know that He is always present in a believer's life, we just seem to have trouble recognizing it. Perhaps it's because the quiet moments of faith's ride are when we hear Him best. His word does promise, "Be still and know that I am God."

One of my favorite scriptures is Psalm 23:2–3: "He makes me to lie down in green pastures; He leads me beside still waters, He restores my soul." As a professional artist the past thirty years, I have painted many different scenes from around the world and most all of them seem to evoke a feeling of peacefulness or serenity to the viewer. Perhaps it is because I love to paint calm, reflective water or gentle pastoral scenes. Hopefully, it goes deeper than that and is a fruit of His Spirit in my life. I believe that any believer, who makes himself available to the Prince of Peace, will in some way, reflect and project some of His marvelous attributes. As an artist, I also know that we need to approach any painting or creative endeavor with expectation. If we begin with a hopeful spirit and let the peacefulness of the process guide our hands, the results are usually more satisfying and successful.

Challenges, mistakes and unforeseen events may occur along the way, yet we need to look for the good that can come of them. In painting we sometimes call them "happy accidents." A slip of the brush, a wrong choice of color, or paint that drips where we didn't want it, can often turn into something that enhances the painting. God's word gives us a similar lesson for life in Romans 8:28 (NKJ) when He says: "And we know that all things work together for good to those who love God, to those who are the called according to His purpose."

So, as I travel, whether it's on vacation, business, or life in general, this artist has learned to start with a positive and expectant attitude and face every challenge along the way with a Romans 8:28 kind of attitude. The next story is from a journal I took while traveling across country on vacation. Before my husband and I left, we purposed in our hearts to make the journey a prayerful one. From the very beginning, things happened which threatened to sabotage our trip and our joy along the way. You will see how God used them to bring blessings in unexpected places and ways.

God Is

Like a verse that comes in unexpected time
Expressing your emotions with rhythm and rhyme,
Or a song that wells from the deep of your heart
And joy like a wave swells on from the start,
God Is.

You sought Him often during trials and struggles in life
Pleading your case for answers to strife
Yet the silence was deafening,
His voice was in mute.
Faith's answer was "no" or "wait"
And perseverance made you more astute.

And just when you thought
He was busy elsewhere
When you stopped pushing and prodding
To see if He cared.

When the dust was settled, the grass was green
And trials ahead were yet unseen.
With timeliness that can only be His,
God spoke when least expected for
God Is.

Iris Carignan

Expect the Unexpected

"Is the spirit of the Lord restricted? Are these His doing?" (Micah 2:7b). "And we know that all things work together for good to those who love the Lord, to those who are called according to His purpose" (Romans 8:28).

The flashing electronic sign read "Expect Delays." Roadwork lay ahead. "Now you tell us, Lord!" I mumbled to myself. This clue could have been helpful if we had seen it before leaving on our epic journey across America. Now that we were home and still assimilating all that had occurred during the past few weeks, I couldn't help wonder what other signs we may have missed before our summer trip.

Our ultimate goal for the journey had been a family reunion in Georgia, my birthplace. It had been about sixteen years since I had been back and we had decided to drive instead of fly so we could also sightsee along the way. Fond childhood memories of traveling that route with my family had painted a rose colored picture in my mind's eye. Now, gazing with enlightened hindsight, the rearview mirror of the past was tinted with some new colors. Perhaps we also could have used a sign that read: "Expect the Unexpected".

On May 9, 2014, we had set out towards our Southeastern goal across country. With a wedding to attend in Temecula first and a good night's rest a little further down the road in Palm Desert, we had hoped to get a jump start on our long journey the next day. Little did we know, our trip would hit a major detour right at the get-go. Energized by a hearty breakfast and good night's rest, we strolled outside that Saturday morning with great energy and zest for the trip, only to find that our car had been broken into. The rear window was smashed and I noticed that my large piece of luggage was missing. We had thought ourselves smart by not bringing all of our suitcases into the hotel room the night before. We had each packed a small bag of clothes in prep for the next couple of days and left the remainder in the car. Thankfully, I had brought the camera and my jewelry inside, but the bag that was stolen had contained three weeks of my best clothes for the trip still ahead of us.

Now, three days after our return, I muse about an encounter with a fellow patient at my chiropractor's office. He was requesting an extra appointment in anticipation of a planned blow to his body. This young guy was a stuntman who was preparing to film a commercial and knew that in a few days he was going to experience a major hit by a big burly football player. "Wouldn't it be nice," I turned and said to him, "if we all knew ahead of time when we were going to be hit in life?" I left the doctor's office and started my drive home. The red light turned green at the intersection and the car ahead of me started to proceed, as did I.

Slamming on the brakes, we both came to an abrupt stop as a speeding car raced through a red light in front of us. "Whew! That was a close one." Talk about knowing when you're going to get hit. I'm sure the driver in front of me was also shaken by the close call we both experienced.

Just a Bunch of Clothes

The Trip: Pacing back and forth as the broken glass was being cleaned up, I told myself over and over that it was *"just clothes, material things, not anything really important."* The hotel had "comped" our room and the police officer left after taking our report when suddenly I noticed that another bag was also missing. It was a small tote bag that had belonged to my mother and was filled with a few incidentals. The police officer returned to add the new information to the report. It was then that the "hit" really came. I was describing the small tote bag: "It's black with a picture of the Eiffel Tower and the word Paris on the front. It belonged to my mother (now deceased) who bought it when we traveled together to France in 1999." Tears welled up and threatened to overflow. "Inside was a Bible, a book ('Joni and Ken') and my personal journal."

Emotion barely let me finish my description and the policeman seemed to empathize at that point. I struggled to remember everything else I had put in the tote bag, but it all seemed so insignificant anyway. *Lord, I don't know why this happened and it doesn't feel very good right now, but I praise you anyway.*

Larry dropped me off at a nearby shopping mall while he got the window fixed. We had backtracked about ninety miles to get the repair done. Thank the Lord there was an insurance-approved shop there with just the right window to fit the make and model of our vehicle, on a Saturday, no less! Our GPS system had taken us on a long, circuitous route to the glass repair shop. Even the navigation system seemed to be conspiring against us. The lady's voice kept telling us to get off the freeway. While driving through the back roads of Murrieta, the area seemed very familiar. I began thinking about my mother and father. "Of course," I realized, they had attended a Baptist church in that very area when they lived in Riverside County several years earlier. Remembering our pre-trip decision to pray for the churches and believers of every town, I prayed. Was the "navigation lady" temporarily possessed by a higher power that day?

The usual uplifting experience of shopping was instead very heavy and laden with an overwhelming sense of loss and intrusion. Dragging myself through the colorful collection of "retail therapy", as someone had advised, I ventured towards a section of pretty blouses. Was it my own foggy funk, or had the price tags become wagging tongues? Their high prices certainly seemed to mock my futile attempt to replace three weeks of clothes. Reality set in like a second blow. So many of the clothes taken were brand new, some never even worn. I wanted to run to the nearest restroom and cry. Gathering myself, I proceeded only to find the tears impossible to hold back a few minutes later. They spilled out again while asking a nice lady for directions in the mall and she kindly did her best to comfort me. "I just feel so overwhelmed," I kept repeating. She must have been a believer too, I sensed, as she even offered to help me shop.

Some new clothes, a new piece of luggage to hold them, and the window repaired, we aimed the car towards our original destination and started once again on our journey. *Lord, is this a sign?* "Should we just turn around and go home?" I considered out loud to my husband. This early detour had not only initiated serious thoughts of cancelling our trip, it had set us back by twelve hours. For several miles my mind continued to wander in and out of the lanes of doubt as we pushed forward late that afternoon. My Aunt Valeria and Cousin Lynda, were not going to be there and seeing them had been a key reason for planning this trip. It had been about sixteen years since I'd seen either one of them and at eighty-four, this aunt was the only living sibling of my mother. Would I ever get to see her again? I also veered into the lane of regret because my younger brother and a special cousin and his wife weren't going to be there either. We trudged on despite our troubling start and I said a prayer for whoever stole my bags. *Lord, please encourage the person who stole my things to read the Bible, the inspirational book, my journal, and the devotional that were in the stolen tote bag, that their heart might be changed and their life turned around.*

Looking back now, I see that despite our early troubles, we had experienced many blessings along the three-week route. The reunion had been very successful, with fifty-five people attending and the weather beautiful. We had spent some blessed time at the lake house, where many childhood memories with parents, grandparents and cousins were captured in its rustic charm and peaceful, mossy environment. It was the same place where a jet plane had dropped its fuel tank over my head and into the lake when I was seventeen. It was the same lake where I'd sat for hours and fished, while soaking in the beauty of its serenity and catching its peacefulness in my heart, later manifesting in many of my paintings. Unexpected family bridges were also built as a result of the one aunt not attending.

The highlights of many other wonderful experiences and sights played across my mind as I reminisced about our recent journey. All of these memories now gathered in our hearts as a result of forging onward in the journey to Georgia. They were also sprinkled with several unexpected blessings and encounters along the way. One such blessing was a special anointed time, obviously planned by the Lord. It came just one day after the big bump in the road at the beginning.

Amazing Mother's Day Appointment

Today is Mother's Day. After arriving in Arizona (our first planned stop) at 3 a.m., and sleeping in for much needed rest, we hit the road about noon today. No time to sightsee as we are running twelve hours behind schedule. *If we were at home, we'd probably be at church,* I imagine, *and they would be handing out flowers to all the mothers right about now.* Although I already celebrated with my children and grandchildren before leaving for this trip, I feel like celebrating in some way. Driving another long route would have normally called for casual clothing, but I desperately need to do something festive in light of some lingering depression from the day before. So, I don one of my pretty new blouses this morning and even adorn it with a nice necklace—a gift from my daughter. *Thank you, Lord, that my jewelry wasn't stolen.* The pendant matches the blouse perfectly and the outfit does seem to lift my spirits. *Who cares if I'm a bit overdressed for the road?*

About halfway on route to New Mexico, we stop at a gas station-convenience store named Love's. Immediately we appreciate the clean, cool atmosphere. After buying some beverages, we take advantage of the indoor dining tables and sit down to eat the lunch I packed this morning. While munching on our pimiento cheese sandwiches, a lady enters the store and sits at the table next to us. I glance at her and notice she is a bit overweight, has scraggly hair, lots of tattoos and missing front teeth. I'm ashamed of my instant judgmental impression. She looks right at me and despite my own vain self, I give her a friendly smile. "I like your necklace," she initiates. Our conversation begins and we are quickly becoming friends. We learn her name is Michelle and that she is a truck driver, but has only recently gone *on the road.* "My father spent his life trucking," she tells us, "and I decided to join him so we could catch up on so much of what I missed while growing up." Michelle indicates her heart of faith as she mentions "It was God's timing, and we have learned so much about each other while traveling together." I say something to indicate our mutual faith. She reveals that one key reason she wanted to travel with her dad was her hope to "lead him closer to the Lord."

We finish our lunch and are introduced to Michelle's dad, Roger, who has now joined her. Then, to our astonishment, she walks over to our table and says, "Could we pray together?" So we all stand in a circle, join hands and pray out loud right there in the middle of a convenience store! Wow! Surely this was a God thing.

Stepping Up

This had clearly been God's timing and an appointed encounter. Only He knows if it would have occurred if we hadn't been held up the day before and thus on the road late that day. Clearly we wouldn't have arrived at the convenience store at the same time. Would Michelle have started a conversation if I hadn't worn the unconventionally dressy travel clothes and pretty necklace that caught her eye? What if my own judgmental thoughts had interfered with God's smile on my face? I believe God knew all along. I also think He used this poignant and serendipitous moment to impress upon our hearts the importance of placing value on the right things as we travel on the road of life. He may have even used that moment to bring Michelle's father closer to His kingdom that day as we prayed together in an unconventional place. Psalm 132:16 says: "I will also clothe her priests with salvation." Perhaps the road bump at the start of this journey was actually preparation towards a holy kind of clothing that my Lord wants me to wear so that others might also receive salvation.

Today I attended the first session of a Summer Bible study at my church. It is a Beth Moore study called "Stepping Up, A Journey through the Psalms of Ascent". It is the first of such studies I have done, but it just felt too right not to try it. Ironically, the leader began the morning discussion with the question: "If you were preparing for a trip, what would you pack?" After a few responses from several ladies, the leader then asked: "If you were on your way to heaven, what would you take with you?" Of course, I had to share a little of my recent experience with the theft of my suitcase and all the clothing I'd so carefully packed. "It is such a metaphor," I said. "Sometimes in our journeys in life we may pack what we think we should for the trip and perhaps we may think that we are packing what we should for our final journey to heaven, but God may have other ideas of what is truly important."

Abiding Clothes

My Lord will never leave me
Nor forsake me
He will have favor on my children
If they also follow
His word and obey.

My Lord will reign in my heart
As long as I allow Him and
Give Him place.

Then I am clothed in His righteousness
And I sing for joy.

Let me go once more to His house,
Let me give to the poor and praise
His name.

He gives me clothes of salvation
And songs of joy.
And mine enemies He gives clothes of shame.

By Iris Carignan, 2014 (Inspired by Psalm 132)

Back on Track

Monday, May 12. We are finally on track with our schedule and able to do some sightseeing. Our first landmark is the Carlsbad Caverns in New Mexico. While Larry has never been here, I was with my family at the age of ten. As we venture further into many of the vast, craggy rooms, I see that the caverns are even more beautiful than I remember. Now, stepping into an enormous space seems to open more memories from my first visit as a child. I remember a point in that tour when the guide turned off all the lights to the cave we were in. The darkness was indescribably void of all light. You couldn't see your hand in front of your face. We learned from a guide on this tour that they no longer turn off the lights except for group tours.

In 1Samuel 24:1–4, we read about the time when David was hiding for his life in a cave. Thinking back on my childhood cave memory, it is easy to see why King Saul went into the cave where David was hiding and yet didn't know he was there. David probably couldn't see Saul either, but recognized the king's voice. Perhaps David's more youthful eyes also helped him see a little better, but having had this experience made me well aware of the darkness in such places.

Later in the day I also found myself recalling a vivid and impressive dream I'd had about forty years ago. Not many can remember their dreams from the night before; nevertheless, this one had been so impacting and frightening, that it remains clear even today.

The Dream

In the dream, I find myself in a very dark place. I somehow know that I cannot leave this forebodingly dark space. Every so often, some object seems to bump into an invisible wall or dimension, and when it does, a window opens up, giving a view of the outer world. I look out the "window" and see a world of sunlight and youthful life, but am aware that I cannot go there. Another object bumps the invisible wall and a door shape opens to once again reveal sunlight and life continuing. How can I escape this terrible place, I wonder. My eyes adjust to the darkness and the vague outline of figures slowly takes focus. I mostly sense the presence of other people sitting nearby. I somehow know that they are angry with me. Their souls seem to be screaming at me because I never told them about Jesus and His salvation. I realize that they are all there because I failed to witness to them when they were alive. One of them seems to be a dear relative whom I had only met once before his death.

The dream ends and I awaken, crying desperately for all the missed opportunities and lost souls, past and future. While the memory of that dream has faded some, the passion for evangelism it provoked those many years ago remains a part of my journey's purpose.

It's Tuesday and we are on the road to Dallas, Texas. We got an early start today in preparation for the long seven hour drive. We began on Highway 180 and connected with Highway 20 a short while ago. As we passed through the small town of Seminole, Texas, we started to slow down, but apparently not enough. Larry got pulled over by a cop and ticketed (nothing worse than getting a ticket except maybe having it documented for posterity in a book). In his defense, the speed limit had whiplashed from 75 mph to 35 mph and neither of us had seen the posted school zone sign. Oops! It seems that God is getting our attention right at the start of another day. There He goes again, giving us a metaphor for how we need to slow down and pay attention in life.

The scenery on this route is mostly plain and boring—flat plains, red clay and hay fields on either side of the straight highway. Childhood memories of cross-country trips that included long and tedious passage through Texas brushed my mind like a hot desert wind. En route, we pass through a town called Gail. It wasn't indicated on our map and now, while passing through it, we see why. Even the buzzards circling above seem perplexed as to its value. I found myself wondering how it got its name. Was it named after a girl or was it a misspelling of the gale winds that sweep through it with disaster? Whatever the case, this tiny, nearly non-existent town hardly seemed worthy of any name. Its pitiful sad state seems to be an ominous warning to all who pass through. It's like a metaphoric sign that reads: Caution: Are You Living a Significant Life? I say a prayer of hope for Gail, Texas, though it had no church.

A while down the road, we travel through the town of Roscoe, Texas and thoughts of my maternal grandfather, Roscoe Mathis, come to mind. He was a railroad man and ironically, the first sight greeting us in that town is a railroad station and major R.R. crossing.

After arriving in Dallas later than planned and getting some much needed rest, we had assessed our day and narrowed down our sightseeing plans to only two key places: The Museum of Biblical Art and the George W. Bush Library. It seemed to make the most sense to start at the farthest site and work our way back towards our route to the next destination, so we chose to see the Museum first. What a blessing! About one month before leaving on this, trip a family member had emailed a video about a new mural depicting the resurrection of Jesus. We had noticed that it was on display at that museum, so it was only right to stop by and see it. The stop was well worth our time. Viewing the forty-foot long painting, "The Resurrection," by Ron Di

Ciani, seemed to resurrect our wearied bodies and spirits too. The whole museum was filled with awesome inspiration that energized us for the next phase of our journey.

Our next stop was the George W. Bush Library. Walking inside, we had felt another kind of inspiration and unexpected reflection. Even though it has only been a swift few years, thirteen to be precise, we are stunned to be reminded of our nation's devastating trial on September 11, 2001. President Bush had only been in office about seven months when terrorists had struck the Twin Towers in New York and the Pentagon. I can't help but remember my thankfulness to the Lord for giving us a godly leader to handle this critical national situation. Walking through the Hall of Remembrance for all that died that day was an awesome reminder of the terrible shock and loss.

Precarious Dream

A long forgotten memory of the 2000 presidential election suddenly came flooding back with great clarity. We had all gone to bed the night of the election, believing it was all over after hearing that George W. Bush was the declared winner of the Presidency. That night I had a vivid dream and its meaning was quickly revealed upon awakening. Little did we know that the election was actually hanging precariously. It seems there was some question about ballot counting in Florida due to the "hanging chad" system they used.

The Dream: I dreamt that I was standing outside on my patio and looking at a hanging flowerpot. I noticed that the pot was hanging precariously off kilter. I stood there staring at it and thinking that it needed to be righted. We need to pray, I thought, and began to do so. To my amazement, the flowerpot slowly began to right itself into a level position before my eyes.

I awoke the next morning to the sound of our clock radio blasting the morning news of the unsettled election. Wow! The dream was not only still vivid in my mind, it had instantly been given meaning by a newscaster. Ironically, neither my husband nor I had set the radio to come on, and hadn't put it on for several weeks prior. The interpretation was absolutely clear. I knew instantly that the flowerpot had represented the election and that all believers needed to pray fervently for the outcome of its precarious position. What I didn't know then and what was revealed so shockingly several months later was the full impact of our prayers at that moment in time.

Our nation stood by, watching as the election finally righted itself. While I don't know much about Al Gore, Bush's opponent in that election, I know that this was an election that went through a spiritual battle. I also truly believe His Spirit, through our prayers, placed the man He wanted at the helm just months before 9/11.

After one night in Vicksburg, Mississippi, and a brief tour of an historical Civil War site, Georgia is not only on our minds—we have finally arrived! We drove up to my brother's house later than we hoped and it was so good to rest awhile and visit with family. We all agree to just rest up the next day and visit some more before heading further south to Albany and the lake house.

The lake house looks better than ever as we round the bend of the dirt road. My cousin did a remodel a couple of years ago and it's the first time we've seen the results. Fond memories flood my mind as we take inventory of the changes. I venture out to where the sleeping porch used to be and instantly, nostalgic sounds muse in my mind's ear. The wonderful yet frightening sounds of hard rain tap dancing on the tin roof; thunderous storms flashing across the sky, all evoke a kind of comfort. My brother and his wife arrive a few hours later and we agree that the fresh change to the cabin is appealing. My sister-in-law, there for the first time, is especially impressed after hearing about a "very rustic" place. One very countrified memory still lies in the recesses—an outhouse we used until the day plumbing came to this simple abode. I'm glad things worked out for all of us to stay here during our reunion in Albany. It will be a good way to visit some more. By now, my southern accent has kicked back in and flows as natural as the Flowing Well that the lake club was named for. "Y'all want to sleep in this bedroom or do you want to be in the new loft? I'm fixin' an easy dinner and there will be plenty for all ya'll in awall (awhile)," I said as naturally as I did in my youth.

The reunion is a big success with about fifty-five attending and some great connections and re-connections. That evening, my brother and his oldest son and grandson do some fishing. Larry and I and my sister-in-law choose to relax and enjoy the cool spring evening at the lake house. Having the opportunity to talk with my sister-in-law is a rare blessing. She shares her disappointments regarding some family trials and I feel thankful and honored that she is willing to open her heart. I see the look of disappointment and despondence on her face. "How come ya'll never had any big problems with your kids?" I give her a way-too-pat answer that doesn't paint a complete picture of our child raising history.

All Things Work Together

It's Sunday and another Willie Nelson kind of day as we head out *on the road again* for the return trip home. After some goodbyes and lots of hugs, we resolve that this has been a good visit and we must come back again soon. With Larry driving, I make a cell phone call to my cousin Ray, who set things up for our stay. "Thank you so much. We had a great time and you did an excellent job on the cabin remodel," I say gratefully. My brother calls a little while later to say that he also called our cousin to say thanks. He then tells me that our kind, appreciative words for Ray's good cabin caretaking seemed to touch him greatly. We are all now invited to use it any time we want. What an answer to prayer! My brother had expressed some hurt feelings about limited access to the family cabin over the years. It seems that a bridge has been built that may not have happened if my aunt had come. "All things work together for the good" (Romans 8:28).

A few hours down the road, I find myself thinking of the conversation we had the night before and the pat answer I'd given my sister-in-law. Why did I tell her that we'd never had any serious problems with our kids? Was it because the kind of problems we had were so different than hers? Was it just that things had improved and there was healing with the one child, that it didn't occur to me? Whatever the reason for my momentary dementia that night, I knew I needed to rectify the perfect family impression I'd left. *Lord, help me find a time to talk to her again, that it might be a more genuine testimony and encouragement to her.*

We arrive in Nashville late in the afternoon and settle into our hotel suite. Our time in Nashville and Memphis, Tennessee was delightful. We saw some interesting sites, had some delicious

BBQ, and watched a good Elvis impersonation show. Visiting the Grand Ole Opry house and nearby Opry Grand Hotel in Nashville, as well as Graceland in Memphis, was terrific. I even had the opportunity to sing on stage at the Grand Ole Opry house. Bragging about it now that I'm home has been lots of fun, especially when I get to the part where I say: "I really did sing on stage at the Grand Ole Opry."

"And it was beautiful!" Larry remarks every time.

"But" I qualify after the appropriate time lapse, "there were about 20 other people on stage at the same time that day too. I'm the only one in that *tour group* who stepped up and sang one phrase of 'America the Beautiful.'" So I can honestly say I sang on stage at the Grand Ole Opry.

The Best Blessing

The best blessing in Nashville was a quick visit with a friend who had recently moved to the area. Joann had been my walking buddy for several years during the time she lived in California while taking care of her aging mother. After her mother passed away, my friend had moved to Tennessee to be with other family. We met up for lunch in downtown Nashville and got caught up on things. She told me she was attending her brother's church and enjoyed it, even though "it's different than mine." *Thank you Lord!* She was still in my prayers often. While I hadn't considered her to be a close friend, our walking times had been special and I always remembered the first day we met and her open invitation to come over for coffee. Now, as we said our goodbyes, my friend choked back tears revealing her heart towards me. Perhaps I had touched her life as well.

It's Wednesday, May 21. We're barely one hour into our drive to Branson, Missouri and the traffic is suddenly moving at a snail's pace. Oh no! It must be an accident. It's probably a big rig holding things up, I complain. It's gonna take us all day at this rate! About ten more excruciatingly slow miles down the road, we see it. It's not an accident at all. No. Everyone is rubbernecking at the tornado damage visible alongside the road. Just a few weeks earlier, it had sliced through the small town along the highway, leaving a path of destruction. Guilt over my earlier complaining sets in quickly. Forgive me, Lord, and please help the people of that town.

As I read my own words of traffic jam frustration, the thought crosses my mind that it is so like us: So like us to complain at the first sign of trouble; so like us to imagine that somebody's carelessness is causing our discomfort; so like us to think of our own difficulty at the moment before considering what pain or trouble someone else may be experiencing. It is also a reminder of how our journey will often involve storms along the way; some of them are storms that wreak havoc in the lives of others.

Unexpected Song

Our road trip to Branson, Missouri got us here at 9:30 p.m. last night, so the late sleep-in and hearty breakfast energized us for today. Tonight we went to a delightful musical variety show. Before the show, we tried to eat dinner at a nice restaurant nearby, only to find it was too busy to accommodate us in time for the show. Instead, we ate at a grungy restaurant across the street from the theater. I resisted nausea while observing the dilapidated, environment and perusing the limited menu. We both decided on the meatloaf, the safest choice. Thirty minutes later our tummies growled with hunger as we looked with delight and trepidation at our generous piles of meatloaf. The food was unexpectedly delicious. We asked for a take-out box and left with enough for two days of meatloaf sandwiches. God had provided and even multiplied our bounty for the next road trip.

I awoke this morning with an unusual dream still vivid in my mind (probably effects of the meatloaf). It was about my great-grandfather, yet running through it was a new song playing over and over. I can still hear the words and melody in my head, so while it is fresh, I must write it down. In about thirty-five minutes, the new song is written with a couple of verses added to the original dream words and a chorus that completes the musical melody perfectly. My smart phone is a great tool for recording this new melody before it disappears into the vast empty space of my brain. The recurring verse that came in the dream included the words: "Down on Highway 59." It is a typical Country Western style song with a story about lost love and a woman who is stuck at a diner, still waiting for her true love to return. I'm amazed that it's a Country Western song (not my favorite musical genre). Even stranger is the sappy story that doesn't reflect me or my life.

We arrive at a beautiful wooded resort called the Cedar Creek Lodge. It's a recommended day trip previously discovered by some friends who had visited the Branson area. After checking out the lush grounds, we settle for lunch at one of the cottage style restaurants on site. The view of the lake below is breathtaking! We strike up a conversation with a couple sitting next to our table. They are feeling some anxiousness regarding recent medical troubles of both their parents and we learn we have some things in common. We find out they used to live in a community near our home and at another time had also lived in Colorado Springs, where we own a business. Before long we are bowing our heads in prayer together and lifting up their parents and the needs that lay heavy on their hearts. Wow! Another God appointed time and connection in a faraway place.

It's our last night in Branson, so we choose to go to the restaurant we had attempted to eat at the night before. The food is very good and we are impressed with our waitress, who goes out of her way to make us happy. Something about her demeanor tells us she may be a believer too, so we ask. Yes she is. "My name is Angelica," she answers us, but "I'm no angel," she declares quickly. After our meal, we ask if we can pray for her in any way. "Yes" she says. "Pray that I will have a better attitude." She goes on to tell us of a customer who left without paying their bill or leaving a tip. Apparently, Angelica felt that her anger over the situation was not Christian. I was impressed and humbled with her attitude that didn't reflect how I might have handled the same situation. She seemed much more angelic than her own assessment. I pray for her silently as we drive back to our hotel.

The dream song is still playing in my mind, so before hitting the bed, I Google Highway 59 to see if such a highway even exists. I have the worst sense of direction, very limited knowledge of any and all highways and can barely tell you which road to travel in my own home state. I asked Larry if he knew of a Highway 59 and where it might be, but he didn't know either. On a hunch and because the song mentions something about being at the "borderline", I try the state of Texas first. What! No way! There's a Highway 59, north to south, and ends right at the border of Mexico. That's amazing. Not only does it go down to the border, but it then becomes another highway. How did my little brain know that? This has to be a gift given for a purpose. I've done quite a bit of singing in my time, but I don't know how to read music or play an instrument.

It's been more than two months since our journey to Georgia and it took me this long to realize the spiritual significance to the song Down on Highway 59. I woke up this morning with the song on my mind again, but this time it wasn't so much the melody that roamed my thoughts, but the message. It was so far removed from anything in my life. First of all, it was a country western style song—not my cup of tea. Second: it was about a woman whose lover or "baby" had abandoned her or left her waiting—not my story after forty-five years of happy marriage. Third: She's on a highway I've never been on; never even heard of until the dream came. Fourth: She is stuck in unrealistic hopes of life. Yet something gnawed at my spirit all night and continues to pester me this morning.

The song tells of a woman who sits in a diner, at a table in the corner, waiting for her love to return. Do we also sometimes put ourselves, and God, in a corner where we can't really see anyone or face the truth? Are we like the infirm man whom Jesus asked, "Do you want to be made well?" Was this a metaphor for all of us who can get stuck emotionally and spiritually while on the highway of life? Is she really a picture of how, as Christians, we keep going to the Lord's table, yet don't fill ourselves with the spiritual foods He has to offer? No, we sit there for days, weeks, even years, sipping on a little of His wine to help ease the pain.

Just two days ago, while at a prayer–study group, we had come to the portion of the study guide where we are invited to "feast at the Lord's table." A list two pages long showed all the attributes of the Savior available to us as His children. We had to examine ourselves and see how many of the Lord's spiritual blessings we were feasting on and how many we were just sampling. The list included things like forgiveness, grace, love, mercy, redemption, joy, etc. I had gone through the long list and realized that for the most part, I had just been sipping on most of them. I was aware of all of them, yet had never fully feasted on all of them and certainly wasn't "feasting" on them now. No, they mostly sat in the back roads of my mind, waiting for me to put them on the plate of my hungry soul and devour them in all their richness. I had treated them more like samples at my local Costco that I tasted now and then.

Down On Highway 59

Last table in the corner,
Down on highway 59
That is where my baby left me,
When he crossed the borderline.

Said he'd come and get me later
Said he was my Valentine
B'fore he left me at the table
Down on Highway 59.

Guess I'll wait here for my baby
Guess I'll have another wine
At the table in the corner
Down on Highway 59.

Yes I know he isn't coming
Yes, I know it's past the time
It's gettin' late here at the diner
Down on Highway 59.

I'll be back again tomorrow
Save my seat just one more time
At the table in the corner
Down on Highway 59.

Maybe it's still just a memory
Sealed in timeless lover's rhyme,
Where I cannot face tomorrow,
And find comfort every time.

Could have found another lover
Could have given up this one
But it's nice here in the corner
Where I don't see anyone.

Yes I know he isn't coming
Yes, I know it's past the time
It's gettin' late here at the diner
Down on Highway 59.

Last table in the corner
Here I am just one more time
I'm still waitin' for my baby
Here on Highway 59.

Music and lyrics by Iris Carignan

Wow! This isn't just a sappy, silly, love song and it is about me in more ways than I'd like to admit. Instead of feasting at the Lord's spiritual table, I sometimes sit at some crummy diner and nibble on the junk food of our culture. The diner may take the form of a movie or a shopping spree. It may look more like a hobby, creative passion or even Christian fellowship, but upon close examination, it may just be junk food for my soul, or at best, just a sampling of all He has in store for me.

Make the Most

Ephesians 3:20 (NIV) says "Now to Him who is able to do immeasurably more than all we ask or imagine, according to His power, that is at work within us, to Him be glory in the church and in Christ Jesus throughout all generations forever and ever Amen!" We keep approaching the throne and asking but not really hearing, receiving, or acting on His provision, promises and precepts. How many times have we prayed about something and God answered, yet we did not see it? Perhaps it wasn't revealed to us clearly then. Maybe we were just so caught-up in our own thoughts, worries and desires, we didn't see it. Maybe we were like the woman in the song who keeps going back to the diner and sitting at the same table in the corner. Maybe we approach God's table and like her, just sit there, sipping the fruit of God's vineyard or drinking the coffee of revival, only to slumber and wallow again. Do we often put ourselves and God in a corner where we can't face the truth? Ephesians 5:15 (NIV) says, "Be careful then, how you live, not as unwise but as wise making the most of every opportunity, because the days are evil. Therefore, do not be foolish, but understand what the Lord's will is."

It's Saturday and we are heading toward Oklahoma City today. After arriving, we stop for our only sightseeing in this town—the Museum of Art. We enjoy a beautiful exhibit of Gilhuly glass sculptures and photography by Ansel Adams before going to our hotel. For dinner we decide on a place called Shorty Smalls.

We arrive in the nick of time, as a storm rolls in with pouring rain, lightning and thunder. The electric storm causes the power to go out for about a minute and we wonder if we will be able to get any hot food for our journey weary bodies. Praise the Lord, the power is back on and the food delivered to our table a short while later. It is scrumptious! I had chosen to have a light meal of soup and salad, while Larry had the BBQ pork entrée. It sure looked delicious, but having had more food than exercise the past couple of days had my stomach feeling overloaded. Larry gave me a few bites for taste and it was indeed the best BBQ so far on our trip. We chat awhile with our very efficient waiter named Chester and thank him for his wonderful and expedient service. We also ask him if there is anything we could pray about for him. "Oh, there are just too many things. I couldn't say," he responds. "Well, just tell us one thing," we prod, but Chester never does give us one thing to pray about. We determine to pray that God will bring a special friend into his life who will show him God's grace and love.

As I read my travel notes about our experience with Chester, it reminds me that too often we get bogged down with troubles. We may even be so weighed down with trials, that we don't know where to begin to ask for help. We had learned from the manager that Chester, our waiter, had been a faithful server for many years and was in fact one of his best waiters. We had sensed that he wasn't a believer, but also sensed that he did indeed have a lot of troubles in his life, yet he served others well. It also occurs to me that my own overloaded stomach was much like me when it comes to serving the Lord. Every day and every week, my Lord fills me with His love and blessings, yet if I don't give to others out of my bounty, I become bogged down much the same as my system does. In other words, we need to exercise the gifts God gives us so that we can come back to His table and feast again, so that others will also be blessed.

Travel Mercies

It's Sunday and we are back on the road again. Whoa! A pick-up truck suddenly pulls out in front of us before we can even get out of the hotel parking lot. *Thank you for your mercy!* Now we find our way to Interstate 40, which should take us most of the way to Santa Fe, New Mexico—our next stop. Most of the clouds have lifted as we leave Oklahoma City, but the drab clouds of a depressed town seem to hold its spirit in captivity. I pray for the town as we head out. I pray again for Chester and I pray for the light of God's love to shine in that city. After a couple of hours on the road, we encounter a large big rig that is weaving all over the place, so we call 911 to report it. Just after that we pass through a small town in Texas called Groom. We stop at a site we had learned of before the trip. It's right alongside the Highway, but in the middle of nowhere. There, marking the site, is a gigantic white cross. After parking, we take a self-guided walking tour through the Stations of the Cross sculptures and the amazing artistic tribute to our Lord's sacrifice and suffering. We learn that all of the sculptures and the cross, were donated by the artists. It is a beautifully inspiring journey within our journey. It also happens to be Sunday and feels like the perfect worship opportunity for us as we travel.

After that refreshing stop and another short break further up the road for our picnic lunch, we head out on I-40 again. It isn't too much later that we see another big rig swaying across the highway lines. We pass as soon as possible and I consider calling in another report to the highway patrol, but realize we've passed too quickly to get the needed information. I look closely at the truck driver as we pass and see a man with his eyes closed. He must be a weary traveler.

Later that evening while settling in at our hotel, we turn on the news. They report on a terrible accident on I-40 West (the highway we were just on). We learn that a big rig hit an SUV, killing a passenger and severely injuring the driver. They suspect that the truck driver was asleep at the wheel. The report goes on to say that the man killed was a well-liked comedic actor. *Oh Lord, have mercy!* Was it the same driver we saw but didn't report? They flash a photo of the driver and he looks all too similar to the man I saw with his eyes closed.

Santa Fe Push

Thankfully, we'd made it safely to our next destination in Santa Fe, New Mexico, but the regrets I felt as I watched the news that night were hanging on pretty tight. We also had some anxious moments as we exited Highway 40 to Highway 25 on our way to Santa Fe. We weren't clear if that was the route we were supposed to take at that point. I was doing the driving and glanced at the gas gauge about twenty minutes into that turn. The tank was very low. My eyes searched this desolate area for miles with hopes of spotting a gas station, but none appeared on the horizon. Aside from an occasional house along the way, this winding desert road offered little hope for fueling up. Memory of a friend who found himself in a similar situation years ago came to my mind as I prayed silently. It had to be at least twenty-nine years ago that a friend in our home Bible study had told us about running out of gas while on a long, hilly desert road.

Hank prayed God would get him to the top of the next hill so he could coast down the other side and make it to a gas station. Unfortunately for our friend Hank, when he got to the top of the hill, he found a long, flat plateau, so no coasting down. He eventually ran out of gas and I don't remember how he got rescued. All I could think about was making my prayer count. I prayed that we would make it to a gas station and not run out of gas. We did make it, thank the Lord. I kept watching the gas gauge all along, and I swear, at some point it stopped moving down! When we drove into the station it was still at 1/8 of a tank—the same as it was 10–20 miles back. Whew!

I wonder why we often pray up to a point of need, rather than the full need. Do we think that if God can just get us that far, we can handle the rest? Is it because some of us don't feel worthy of asking for what we need? Of course, none of us are worthy, but our God is bigger than our weakness and shortcomings and He wants to show us His love and power in all situations.

Something is Missing

Santa Fe is a clean and quaint pueblo-themed town. The old historic Catholic church at the end of the town square is beautiful on the outside; the other town church has an amazing floating staircase inside with a story to tell. Something seems to be missing though. We sense the spiritual difference between this place and many of the places we have visited the past several days. Neither of the two town square churches or the city itself seems to host the Holy Spirit.

After a nap and drive in the town's hillside community, we opt to skip dinner and just go for a dessert treat. Our hotel reception lady recommends a restaurant in the town square as having "really good desserts". I order the chocolate cake a la mode and Larry has the carrot cake—his favorite. "Ugh! This has to be the worst cake I've ever tasted," we chime in unison. We are mystified that the hotel lady thought this place had the "best desserts in town." Maybe this is where the expression "get your just desserts" started, because the cakes here are truly just dessert. Oh well. Seems that the sweet Spirit of God isn't the only sweet thing missing in this town.

Our visit to Santa Fe had also included some time at an art museum and a few art galleries, which I enjoyed. It appears to be a relatively affluent and well-planned community. There was an obvious influence in the town of the many Native Americans who had dwelt there throughout history. I couldn't help but wonder if their ancient religious, pagan and animistic beliefs still filled the air and influenced the town's spirit.

I also began sensing a spiritual difference between the East and West coast of our nation, intangible, and more of a feeling or mood. I noticed that the closer we got to the west coast, the further removed God's presence seemed to be. There was even a large church just outside the town square that had a "for sale" sign on it. If this was a movie and we were characters in a story, the thunderstorm in Oklahoma City the day before would have been ominous warning of impending gloom. We prayed for God's light to break through the darkness of these towns.

We arrived in Scottsdale, Arizona in the early evening, so took a walk into town for dinner. It was absolutely delicious, but the hundred degree heat late into the evening was stifling, so after a short walk around the town square, we collapsed in our luxurious hotel bed for the night.

Today, despite the scorching heat, we venture onto a tour of Frank Lloyd Wright's house called Taliesin West, which is fascinating. After lunch we are on the road again for our last stop on this journey.

Last Stop

Palm Desert is the bookend to this trip and we settle in at our timeshare resort for three days this time. The first day is for respite. We go swimming and so does Larry's cell phone. Despite all efforts to revive it with rice and drying time, it is dead. What is it about this town that seems to eat our things? The second day in Palm Desert, I go into the exclusive El Paseo Drive area and check out an art gallery where I once exhibited my paintings. As I walk in the gallery, I notice several paintings sitting on the floor and many empty walls. I see the gallery owner and inquire. He tells me that the gallery is closing. Oh well, there goes any hopes of showing there again. It saddens me to see any business fold, especially an art gallery of such high quality.

Back at the resort, I think about my sister-in-law and our conversation on the lake last week in Georgia. A prayer first, then I call her. I'm so glad she answers, giving me a chance to say things I regret not having said. We have a blessed time of connection over the phone and I am told that all of her prayer concerns since our visit have been answered. The best part of our talk comes when I am able to share some of my own heartache regarding one of my children. She seems both surprised and glad to know that even devoted believers have struggles and imperfections. I encourage her and we pray together over the phone. Amazing!

After three relaxing days, we check out of the resort and head for home. Larry's cell phone still has no sign of life and this town seems a little dead too.

Our three-week journey is now over. Boy, did it go by fast! Isn't that just the way it goes? We spend weeks planning a trip, then weeks on the trip, yet when it is all done it feels like it all passed by so quickly—a lot like our life's journey, too? We make plans, go through our lives and the closer we near the end, the faster it seems to arrive. As we near the end of a trip, we also feel tired and ready for rest. Those of us who are privileged to live long lives may also feel ready for a "rest."

Open the Word—Close the Journal

Much like my preface in this book, our journey had some roller coaster ups and downs along the way. This journey began with a wedding celebration for a daughter of a close friend. It was a joyous high that quickly got jerked down with the shock of a burglarized car and stolen clothing. A day later, we were up again in the heavenly atmosphere, experiencing an amazing connection with strangers in a convenience store. Along the highways we made new friends, reconnected with some family, ate some good food and saw some relational bridges built along the way. We also saw some marvelous sites and stayed in some beautiful places.

I'm glad for our return home and to enjoy rest. I'm also glad we have our rest in Jesus at the end of our life's journey. Shortly after our return, the father of the bride whose wedding we'd attended at the beginning, passed away suddenly. While we grieve his loss, we celebrate the rest he is now receiving at the end of his journey.

I open the Bible randomly as I close this journal and begin reading in Matthew 6. My eyes scan a few verses and settle on Matthew 6:25. It reads: "Therefore I tell you, do not worry about your life, what you will eat or drink; or about your body, what you will wear. Is not your life more important than food, and the body more important, than clothes? Look at the birds of the air; they do not sow or reap or store away in barns, and yet your heavenly Father feeds them. Are you not much more valuable than they? Who of you by worrying can add a single hour to his life? And why do you worry about clothes? See how the lilies of the field grow. They do not labor or spin. Yet, I tell you that not even Solomon in all his splendor was dressed like one of these. If that is how God clothes the grass of the field, which is here today and tomorrow is thrown into the fire, will he not much more clothe you, O you of little faith?"

Wow! Giving me this verse now couldn't have been more appropriate. I have read it many times and believed it, but my God has surely impressed it upon my heart now. "Let your priests, O Lord God, be clothed with salvation, and let your saints rejoice in goodness." 2 Chronicles 6:41 is another verse He has spoken to me lately. Just yesterday our pastor spoke about taking off the old and putting on the new. How much more timely could that have been?

Colossians 3:5–14 explains further how we should clothe ourselves with things like "compassion, kindness, humility, gentleness and patience." These are the kind of clothes we should put on every day and the kind of clothes that a thief cannot steal. Moreover, we can bring them with us on our last journey home.

Dressing for the Season

The trees are dressed in blossoms
Do you see?
And some are dancing in the breeze,

Their outfits new and clean.
The leaves of green don't mean a thing if we
Would put them on.
Some folks tried it once,
But now they are long gone.
They thought if they could cover-up the shame
they felt inside
In the beauty of the branches,
Their sin could surely hide.

With summer gone and this of course the fall,
The color of their wardrobe
Seemed glorious to all.
But soon the dry and weathered leaves
upon their flesh did itch,
And they heard the footsteps of the Lord
And behind the trees they ditched.

With each crunch and crackle,
As He stepped into the garden;
They knew somehow the season had changed
And with winter things would harden.

But look, they said, upon that hill
A new tree has grown!
It's spring again
And from its' branch new life
Can now be sown

By Iris Carignan

Epilogue to a Journey of Expectations

Two years had passed since our "epic journey" across country to Georgia and back. Since then, another vacation took us to Montana and Wyoming to visit Yellowstone and Glacier National Parks. While in the Glacier Park area, we were able to connect with Joanne, my walking buddy mentioned in "A Journey of Expectations." In that story, Joanne and I met up while passing through Nashville, Tennessee. She had since moved to her old hometown in Montana, but we had continued to stay in touch. So, about a week before leaving for the two parks, I phoned Joanne to say we'd be coming to Montana and wanted to connect with her again.

During the period of time when Joanne was still in California, we used to have some good spiritual conversations as we walked our dogs together. After her move away from California, I often thought about her whenever I walked my dog. I admired Joanne for her feisty spirit and fortitude, especially because she battled a serious medical condition. So I would say a prayer for my absent walking buddy. I felt bad that I couldn't be there to walk with her anymore, and began to pray that God would send her a new friend, a friend who would come alongside her and who would help her know His love and salvation. I knew that she was somewhere in Montana now, but not sure how close to where we'd be.

"Do you live anywhere near Glacier National Park," I asked.

"It's right in my back yard." She replied with enthusiasm. She also told me she was now living in an assisted living facility to help her with her increasing medical needs.

We set a tentative day to meet, but her speech problem made it difficult to understand exactly what her address was, or the name of the place where she now lived. I decided to wait until we were in her area to get an exact address. After arriving in her area, I called her again but couldn't reach her. After several failed attempts, I decided to Google all the assisted living facilities in the area, hoping to nail down a few possibilities. I figured there weren't a lot of them in that small town, but to my surprise there were about 39. I scrolled through all of the names of these facilities and every time I did, one facility seemed to stand out as if it was highlighted. Something (or someone) told me that it was her place. After a few more failed attempts to reach her, I decided to try that one and - bingo! That was it. They couldn't give me her number, of course, so we just dropped by. She was surprised and thrilled to see us, then we learned she had lost her cell phone about two weeks prior. No wonder she didn't answer our calls. Timmy, her large Pyrenees dog, greeted us with recognition and tail-wagging enthusiasm. His eyes seemed to say: "Did you bring my old pal Caesar?"

The next day we stopped by again and took Joanne out to dinner. We had a great time catching up on things and even talked quite a while about spiritual matters. Then she told me she had a new friend. She said she and the new friend often spend long hours talking about things—spiritual things, and that she was a strong Christian. Then she told me her new friend's name. It was *Iris*.

Wow! God not only answered my prayer to bring Joanne a new friend who was a believer, He brought her another Iris. Growing up with this unusual name, I knew how uncommon it was and marveled at God's amazing and ironic ways.

Chapter 9

Seeing Miracles, Signs and Wonders

Amazing Signs at Journey's End

February 2012 is drawing to a close and the rhythm of Mom's breathing seems in tune with winter's passing breezes. I mention to friends this difficult time and how she is nearing her end. At eighty-six, "she has lived a long and full life," someone quips, but such comments by well-meaning friends do little to comfort.

"That doesn't make it any easier," I snap back, tears welling in my eyes and the eyes of my friend also. Winter's wind never stung so cold as the piercing slice cutting its way through my futile hopes. *My maternal grandmother lived to be ninety-two, surely Mom will live as long as her,* I think to myself. Sadly, cancer's reality is quickly snatching that possibility away and Mom is on her final journey.

Since moving Mom into our home, I have witnessed a steady decline in her strength and general health. I heard her talking to someone a few minutes ago, and now she seems to be talking to God again. Of course, I know there is no one in the room with her, but the baby monitor next to her bed gives me full volume of every conversation, real or imagined. She seems to be crying now, so I walk softly into her room to see if she is all right. Her pleading to the Lord stops abruptly as my face rounds through the doorway and my eyes meet hers. Tears on her cheeks betray her statement that "everything is fine."

Our youngest son, Gavin, and his family just arrived to visit one last time. Mom's face lights up as they enter the room. We wheel Mom into the kitchen and up to the table. She turns her head to speak to someone only she can see, and invites the invisible person to join us.

It's now Saturday morning. Gavin and his family will be leaving this afternoon for their long drive back home. Larry is out of town until late Sunday night and I'm exhausted, since I didn't get much sleep last night. The whole night was filled with one-sided conversations broadcast over the baby monitor and keeping my body from much needed rest. Gavin and his wife, Riki, go for a walk after breakfast and I wheel Mom into her room for a nap. As I help her onto the bedside toilet for necessary business, she panics and falls. My grandsons come running to help and we clean up the mess together after settling Mom in comfortably.

It is now about 2 p.m., Gavin's family has left and I hear Mom in distress, so I run to tend to her needs. She motions to get up and I help her, only to see her begin vomiting. This isn't good. After she seems calmed and settled again, I get on the phone to my newly hired assistant.

"Please, Dora, can you come spend the night tonight? Larry is out of town and Mom isn't doing well, she fell and..." I sigh in great relief at her positive response.

"Now, just turn off the baby monitor and get some sleep tonight. I'll sleep in the room with your mom, so don't worry about anything." Dora reassures me.

"Thank you. Promise you'll wake me if anything happens."

It is Sunday morning. I glance at the clock on our bathroom vanity—6:45 a.m., yet I feel refreshed. *Thank you for a good night's rest*, I pray silently. Flipping the baby monitor back on, I hear Mom still talking. She's probably been talking for forty-eight hours straight, but this time I hear something new. *What's this?* She is talking with her Southern accent and whomever she is talking to, she seems to be catching them up on things. "I've been doing.... and Iris has been..." she continues. Mom was born in the South and for years we always knew when she was talking on the phone to someone back home because her accent would kick in. I feel like I'm eavesdropping on her private conversation, so I turn the monitor back off, finish getting dressed and proceed to the kitchen to make breakfast for Dora and I. Peeking into Mom's room on the way down the hall, I see that she is now sleeping peacefully. *Finally!*

Dora and I chat a bit as we finish breakfast, but I don't say anything about the conversation most recently overheard. Dora turns to me and with all seriousness declares that something happened.

"What happened?" I ask.

"Well, this morning," she goes on, "two women appeared in the room with your mother and I."

"What do you mean? You mean like a dream or something?"

"No" she says "It wasn't a dream."

Dora begins describing the two women down to the details of what they were wearing. One of the women she describes perfectly fits the description of my grandmother—Mom's mom. "What time did you see these two women?" I inquire.

"Well there's no clock in the room so I'm not exactly sure, but probably around 6:45 a.m." Of course, I tell her about the Southern accented conversation overheard at that same time.

It's been nearly three weeks since Mom's oncologist informed me that the cancer had taken on a more aggressive form and she had only about a month to live. This most tender yet difficult time is tearing at me. My physical strength seems to be holding out okay, but the emotional turmoil is taking its toll. Mom is totally bedridden now, since her fall a few days ago. We spend a few moments reminiscing and I wonder how much to reveal to her. Should I ask her what she wants for her funeral? Should I even tell her that her time is short? Does she already know? After a few more minutes of precious time by her bedside, I go back to my chores, feeling insufficient.

Mom is now in a deep coma-like sleep and hasn't been able to talk, even when awake the past couple of days. I am devastated. No one told me she wouldn't be able to talk in her last days. Just last week she was able to sit outside on the patio in her wheelchair. Watching her rest quietly and contemplatively was a blessing I never would have enjoyed if she hadn't come live with us. *Thank you, Lord, for this time with her.* There was no hesitation in bringing my mother to our house for her final days, even though I felt inadequate to handle this kind of unknown territory. It was a different story several months ago, when my brother and I set her up in an assisted living facility. Mom had refused my offer to live with us then, but she clearly needed more help as her dementia advanced and the cancer also seemed to be getting worse.

It's time to go to sleep and even though my weary body yearns for rest, I lie awake and worry about the coming days. "I just don't know if I can handle seeing Mom die here in our house," I confess to my husband and break down crying.

Thursday morning and I make my usual trek down the hall. Leaning into her room to check on Mom, I am met with astonishing alertness. "Good morning, Iris," she chirps cheerfully, "How are you this morning?" she prods with amazing strength and clarity. I am dumbstruck at the seeming miraculous revival. For two days she had done nothing but sleep and she hadn't been able to talk for two days before that.

Week four, Sunday morning: Mom's time draws closer, yet there is a radiant glow about her that seems to deny death's call. It has been exactly a week since the strange appearance and overheard conversation. Larry and I note that her breathing is very laborious and at times strangely loud, almost grunt-like. We debate whether or not to leave her with Dora, who has arrived to help so we can attend church. Larry advises that it probably would be better to stay home. Mom seems more distressed and we check in on her frequently. I call the hospice folks and report the current situation and they come over quickly.

It's 10 a.m. and Mom has passed. As I watched her spirit depart, I said with final desperation and hope: "Say hello to Jesus for me...and to Dad too!" Words cannot express this acutely personal experience, so I will go no further in this part.

After I have gathered my emotions, the hospice nurse has finished and necessary preparations made, I go to the many boxes stacked in our family room. Fishing through one of them, I pull out an eight by ten inch photo of my grandmother (Mom's mom). For some reason, I didn't have any photos of her anywhere in the house, but many of Mom's things still lay unpacked in our family room, waiting for such treasures as this to be discovered.

I hold up my grandmother's photo to Dora. "Does this look anything like one of the women you saw in Mom's room last week?"

"That's her!" she declares with assurance.

Many believers and non-believers might have a problem with this story. Some might say that my own emotions caused me to imagine it, but remember, I didn't see the women in Mom's room—Dora the caregiver did. I heard Mom speaking in her Southern accent at the same moment Dora saw the appearance. There were no pictures of my grandmother in view anywhere in our house, so her description was uncanny in accuracy.

I remember reading a devotional by Billy Graham last summer that spoke of the passing of his grandmother. He told of her sitting up in her deathbed and seeing and talking to her departed husband. Graham went on to say that he believed that "sometimes God gives His departing saints glimpses of heaven." He also said that these views are also to encourage those of us who are left behind.

Luke 20:36 finds Jesus explaining some things about the afterlife to the Sadducees. In his explanation regarding marriage, Jesus also reveals that in the "resurrection of the dead, they are equal to the angels and are sons of God, being sons of the resurrection." He goes on to say in verse 38: "For He is not the God of the dead but of the living, for all live to Him." In Luke 24: 38–39, Jesus shows himself to his disciples after His resurrection. They are at first afraid, but He shows his wounded hands and feet and says: "Handle me and see, for a spirit does not have flesh and bones as you see I have."

These two verses speak to me in regard to the amazing appearance of that day. I now believe that when a person's soul is so close to the spiritual realm, hovering between the two worlds, they may begin to see with spiritual eyes much like Balaam's eyes were opened for a special time and reason (see Numbers 22:22–33). Mom's eyes were brighter than we had ever seen during her last week with us. Perhaps she was allowed to see some of the glory that lay ahead for her, but I don't know why Dora was also allowed to see the two women, except that it gave encouragement to me. I can only thank my Lord for the miraculous slice of hope that He allowed me to experience as I witnessed the end of a loved one's journey here on earth.

Give My Love to Jesus

Give my love to Jesus, when you get up there
Tell Him that I love Him, still
He should be aware.
That I'm going to miss you, now that you're with Him,
Give my love to Jesus
Till we meet again.

Give my love to Jesus when you're face to face.
Put your arms around Him,
When you're in His place,
Where all who come to visit are received within.
Give my love to Jesus till we meet again.

Music and lyrics by Iris Carignan, 1988

Surprising Fountain of Youth

My dear mother passed away March 4 of 2012. While she would say she earned all of the wrinkles on her face, I would say she had more than the average eighty-six-year old. Perhaps the extra character lines came from hardships she endured. Maybe it was also because at the age of seventy-one, she had lost a considerable amount of weight. Whatever the reason, she laughed at it with good humor and didn't mind the brutally honest queries from little grandchildren who noticed.

When cancer began to take its final toll on my mom, we insisted she come to our house to let us care for her. By the time she moved in, she had lost another ten pounds and was looking quite frail. Her mind wasn't as sharp either, for Alzheimer's had added distress on top of the cancer. Thankfully, she still knew who we were and managed to carry on short conversations pretty well. Doctors had given her about a month.

As her time grew closer, I began to notice how radiant she was becoming. Every morning she seemed to look more and more beautiful, even younger. Of course, I figured it was my imagination; after all, she was my mom. One day my husband said something about it.

"You mean you see it too?" I said.

"Oh yeah!" He said. "She looks younger."

Each new day seemed to bring a more vibrant and radiant glow like I'd never seen in Mom, and each day she did appear younger, yet she continued to lose more weight because she could no longer eat anything. Then, after nearly four weeks, Mom passed away. Hospice was called and the officials had come to take her away, so of course my husband and I went in to say our last good-byes. We both stood in mournful, yet astonished, bewilderment as we visually documented that by the time mom passed, she had lost about eighty percent of her wrinkles.

The verse in Ephesians 5:27 says the church will be presented to Christ at His second coming "without spot or wrinkle." It has long been a favorite of mine and even more so as I look at my own aging face and *claim it* with amused, yet hopeful anticipation. Some have asked me what this small miracle meant, and I always say that God must have been preparing her for His coming and just needed a little head start.

A Stop Along the Way

As I walk along the path of life,
These truths, I have to say,

Are often good to ponder
When I stop along the way.

Their impressions fresh and cool
Like a breeze against my face,

Give my steps a lively lift
And my stumbles gentle grace.

They are the words a mother gives
And even so much more.

They cut the path and pattern
Women were created for.

My mother gave them to me
In the wisdom of her days

So these things I must consider
When I stop along the way

The richness of their value
Are a treasure not to bury.
They fill my heart and shape me,
For the man that I did marry.

And though the autumn colors
Are not too long to stay,
These golden leaves she gave me,
Linger, when I stop along the way.

Iris Carignan

It's All in a Name

A few years ago, I started a business selling a ladies handbag that I designed. This unique handbag, with changeable styles and colors, needed a classy name. So I gave it many weeks of consideration, trying all kinds of words and word combinations. Then one day while at a church missionary reception, we learned of a young orphan girl who needed to be sponsored. I asked what her name was and knew immediately we would become her sponsor. Her name was Villa Rica (pronounced Via Reeka). I also knew that her name was inspiring me down a new path of names for my purse.

I was hoping to use a word which had international recognition and flair. Upon hearing the name "Villa", I thought of the word "Via", which means *the way to*. A week later, while singing to praise music and driving through town, the word "adorn" entered the name arena for my handbag. Yes! That's it! I shouted out loud. "Viadorne" became the name of my new changeable handbag. It was perfect because it described what it was (the way to adorn your purse) and sounded international and classy, too.

Three years into the business, and during a more somber time, I mourned the loss of my mother. While preparing to write Mom's eulogy and rummaging through a large box, I made an exciting discovery. There, underneath mementos, photos, and other memorabilia, was a stack of papers neatly clipped together. It was a handwritten memoir from my maternal grandmother. The top paper began with statistics of its author, her name: Vautez Mathis, her date of birth: January 14, 1906, and other such information.

Then, my eyes fell to the final stat—her place of birth: *Villa Rica*, Georgia. I gasped in amazement at this new revelation. It was the exact same name as the orphan we sponsored and had inspired the name of my handbag. Even though Georgia is my own birthplace, I had never heard of a town by that name and certainly didn't know my grandmother was born there.

In Proverbs 22:1, it says: "A good name is to be chosen rather than riches." God had truly given me a meaningful name for my product, beyond anything I ever imagined. More importantly, He helped my husband and I find our way to sponsoring a beautiful girl in the Philippines.

Beautiful Angel Dream

Several years ago, I had a dream that was so vivid and beautiful, I decided to paint it. It is the only painting of angels I have done thus far. The dream started with me standing outside, looking up. I saw what seemed to be two birds—a white bird and a black bird. The black bird flew off to the west and the white bird started flying down closer to me. I saw that the white bird wasn't a bird but an angel. The angel was waving its arms joyously as if dancing to beautiful music that I couldn't hear. I stood there gazing up, proclaiming over and over, "This is so beautiful! This is so beautiful!" Two more angels appeared behind the first one. They were also joyously dancing and praising God.

As I watched in the dream, an awareness came to me that the two angels in the back were *joined* in some way. The last thing I saw was that the angel on the left (in the rear) was more masculine than the others and had star-like jewels running up his chest and around his halo. The glistening stars were red, white, and blue.

For many weeks afterward, I thought about this beautiful dream and wondered about its meaning. I am not sure what it meant, but felt that the black bird represented evil and it was clear that the male angel, with the red, white and blue glimmering stars on his chest, represented the USA. I think the joining of the back two angels was geographic and perhaps represented America and Mexico. When I decided to paint the dream, I began searching for models. Ironically, the young woman who ended up modeling as the female angel next to the symbolic American angel was a Mexican-American. Even more ironic was her name—*Angelica*. In looking at the painting, you will see the rear two angels share a pair of wings, which represents the "joining of the two".

While I do not know the meaning of the dream for sure, there was a terrible earthquake in California about a month after I had the dream. It's possible the black bird that flew west represented the quake on the west coast. The earthquake was in Southern California, which borders Mexico (our geographic and historic sister). It could possibly be the meaning of the two "joined" angels. In Zechariah 5:9, it tells of angel-like creatures seen in a vision by him. "Then I raised my eyes and looked, and there were two women, coming with the wind in their wings; for they had wings like the wings of a stork."

Astonishing Vision Perspective

Matthew 3 gives us a most amazing account of God's spoken approval and love for His only son when Jesus was baptized by John. It demonstrated an important spiritual principal for all believers. John the Baptist was resistant to the idea of baptizing the one whom he knew to be the Son of God—the Messiah. Jesus insisted, knowing full well the importance of this significant act of obedience to His Father. It was also a pivotal commencement of His mission on earth. His purpose, after all, was to bring salvation through His sacrifice and therefore "wash" us clean or baptize all believers from the sin that condemns us. Yet, He, being the Son of God and in fact God incarnate, was already pure and holy. So, why did He need to do this? While we may not comprehend all that happened in this account, we can certainly gain perspective on its importance in a believer's life. For, if the Lord Himself saw the need to be baptized, then we have no excuse not to be. We also glean from this passage the heavenly Father's perspective on this act. "And suddenly a voice came from heaven saying, 'this is my beloved Son, in whom I am well pleased'" (Matthew 3:17 NKJ).

While rereading this account a few days ago, I recalled a vision I had about twenty years ago. I had just sat down on the couch to relax awhile, when suddenly a vivid and amazing vision appeared right before my eyes. It was a picture of Jesus when He was baptized. The beauty of it was stunning and I was obviously amazed and startled by such a sight. There was a transparency to it, yet it seemed like a 3D movie playing in the air just in front of my eyes. What was even more astounding, if that is possible, is the view of His baptism as the perspective that God the Father would have from heaven. It was as if I was also looking down from the heavens at this marvelous event and seeing it from the Father's viewpoint. In the sight, I saw thousands of shimmering sparkles circling in rings around Jesus' head as He immersed His head and wavy hair in the water. I didn't quite know what to make of this most unusual and surprising experience. I wasn't sleeping or even lying down at the time, but was wide awake. Others were in the room, but only I saw this exquisite picture. Even more oddly, I hadn't read that passage at any time recent to the event.

I'm still not sure why God allowed me to experience this most joyful spiritual milestone, but have added it to my collection of many unexpected and gracious gifts from my heavenly Father. I am also thankful for that brief but poignant taste of God's perspective on how pleased He is when His children are obedient to Him.

Chapter 10

What Others See

Building Relationships

My husband, Larry, had his own construction company for nearly thirty-five years. As a commercial building contractor, his work focused on office buildings, auto dealership facilities, as well as churches and non-profit facilities. Most of his work was in our own community where he built more than just buildings—he built relationships and an excellent reputation. His first project was, in fact, building a relationship with me. We met just after he finished serving in the Seabees division of the military, where he built facilities, barracks, and hangars in Vietnam. Not long after his release of service, he came to California to start his construction business, and that's when we met. But I digress.

The early years of construction were a struggle at times, but he learned much about the business. Unfortunately, when the opportunity to partner with another contractor came, he also learned how *not* to do it. His business partner professed to be a Christian and that added a level of confidence to his new venture. However, his partner's character and trustworthiness failed to match-up to God's standards and Larry discovered firsthand the difference between a stated faith and a true faith in business.

While this was a difficult time for Larry, the lesson learned was a very important one. He knew, better than ever, that he needed to build his life and his business on the "rock" of faith.

As for building our relationship, I couldn't be more blessed. For more than forty-five years, he has continued to build on the love and faith that we share. We both know the importance of letting Jesus be Lord of our life in every area, not just on Sundays.

The Touch

For My Husband on Our 45th Wedding Anniversary

> The touch of your hand
> Is a comfort and great fire
> The warmth of your love
> As a channel of desire
> That flows from within
> A man of great strength
> And comes from Him,
> To you, then me,
> In perfect compatibility
>
> Your hand in mine
> Has a grip that's Devine
> And holds more than amorous sway
> It grasps the source of love's pure line
> And begs my heart to give way.

Your hands embrace
The work of a builder,
Who builds with a passion that's fervent
Using the tools of love and faith,
They embody the heart of a servant.

The touch of my lover
Is gentle and real.
He constructs our life together
With much more than wood or steel.
The hands of my husband
Build up our love so true
For their work and their touch
Were created Lord, by you.

Iris Carignan, 2014

The following two stories are just examples out of many that demonstrate how my husband continued his career in the building industry with integrity, honor and trustworthiness.

Building on the Rock

Over the years, Larry had the honor of building several churches as well as a Jewish temple in our community, but one in particular stands out as a testimony to him. When a local church congregation approached his company to take on a job, it came with a lot of baggage. This church had already experienced failed attempts by two different contractors to build a new sanctuary. Construction had been shut down by the bank that was funding it. Their first contractor had gone bankrupt on them and the second had, as Larry often says, "*Rose to the level of his incompetency.*" After a thorough examination of the building, they uncovered sixty-nine pages of structural corrections that needed to be made.

It was no wonder Larry faced a project fraught with much disarray, disorder and difficulty. At the church construction meetings he quickly learned of other contributing factors that were creating obstacles to the success of the job. He witnessed out-of-control meetings and a general atmosphere of chaos. More importantly, there was no sense of God's leading.

After the second frustrating construction meeting, Larry called the pastor aside. He expressed his sympathies and understanding with their situation and past experiences, and requested a few changes be made. The first thing he suggested probably stunned and humbled the pastor. Larry said, "If you truly want this project to go forward successfully, you need to put it back into God's hands." He went on to say that from that point on they needed to start and end every construction meeting with prayer. Of course, the pastor was on board with these two suggestions. Next, Larry said they needed to trust his leading and not let any committee members (especially one in particular) continue to make changes or call the shots without his and the architect's approval. The third request was that they have an agenda at every meeting.

After these changes were made and the fourth meeting had taken place, the president of the church gave a letter of support and confidence for Larry and his company. In it he said that he felt they were finally headed in the right direction. The church had to raise more funds to proceed with the completion of the sanctuary and this could have potentially caused a major split in the church body. However, they stood strong in faith and only a few church members voted against it.

The project continued and was completed on schedule to the joy of the congregation. When it was all done, the church body was thrilled with the results, and no doubt many had learned a valuable lesson. "Therefore everyone who hears these words of mine and puts them into practice is like a wise man who built his house on the rock. The rain came down, the streams rose, and the winds blew and beat against that house; yet it did not fall, because it had its foundation on the rock" (Matthew 7:24-25 NIV). This congregation of believers surely realized they needed to "put into practice" God's word.

Matthew 7:26–27 goes on to say: "But everyone who...does not put them into practice is like a foolish man who built his house on sand. The rain came down, the streams rose, and the winds blew and beat against that house, and it fell with a great crash." The storms that came their way through two prior contractors could have caused their plans to fail because they had lost their focus of faith. They had forgotten to give it to the Lord. The first two contractors were clearly not following God's word or way in their business practices and were, in essence, building foolishly on their own unstable "sand." Larry came along and set their feet on solid ground again, because he knew the importance of practicing faith in all things.

The new sanctuary became a stunningly beautiful testimony to God's faithfulness to believers who put Him first and practice God's word. It is a house of God that stands strong now because it was truly "built on the rock."

My Favorite Construction Tale

Did you hear about the construction superintendent who had worked for the same developer for many years? He had done a good job for him building houses in many developments. It was his last project before retiring and Joe, the "super," was tired. He told his laborers to "Just slap together the last house." He said not to worry about doing it right, they'd just cover up all the mistakes and shortcuts and no one would know.

The day came when it was done and ready for inspection. He was right. No one caught his cover-ups. His boss, the developer, came by after it passed inspection. "Joe," he said, "You've done another good job. You have been a faithful and good superintendent of mine for many years and I want to thank you for all your hard work. As a thank you gift, here are the keys to the last house. It's all yours."

You Never Know Who's Watching

The construction business is often a precarious line of work. So much depends on the economy, so there were quite a few years along the way that demanded extra diligence and perseverance. Regardless of the construction climate, God continued to bless us with sufficient business and income. At about the twenty-year mark for his company, Larry secured a job doing a remodel of a Saturn car dealership. He had done many different commercial jobs by that time, but this was the first automobile business building.

As the dealership job proceeded, a gentleman showed up, observing its progress. Larry and his crew had no idea who he was and assumed the older man, dressed neatly in a suit and tie, was retired and just enjoyed watching construction.

During the rest of the project, this gentleman continued to visit the job, watching its progress from a short distance away. As the dealership neared its completion, he approached Larry and asked him to send him information about his company. He said his name was Anderson and he had a job that would be starting in several months that Larry might be interested in doing. He handed him a business card with his son's name on it.

It was approximately six months later when Larry's company got a phone call from Mr. Anderson's company. It turned out he owned the Silver Star Automotive Group that included about twelve auto dealers in our town.

Needless to say, Larry's company got the contract, and at its completion, Mr. Anderson's owner rep. commented that it was the "best experience with a contractor they'd ever had."

Over time, that contract led to several more dealership remodels for the Silver Star Automotive Company, as well as some other auto companies. However, they may never have happened if Mr. Anderson had witnessed shoddy workmanship or a poor work ethic while observing Larry and his company. His commitment to integrity, good work and abiding in God, produced "much fruit." Remember also that "since we are surrounded by such a great cloud of witnesses, let us throw off everything that hinders and the sin that entangles, and let us run with perseverance the race marked out for us" (Hebrews 12: 1). Imagine our world if all believers would simply run the race by abiding in Jesus in all we do.

Careful Footsteps

After twenty-five years of marriage, my husband and I decided to celebrate with a cruise to the tropical islands of the Caribbean. While in Jamaica, we decided to go on an adventure climbing up the Dunn's River Falls in Ocho Rios, Jamaica. The giant waterfall has a wide berth and a gradual ascent that has been a popular tourist spot for years. After arriving, we signed up for the "climb" and listened to brief instructions by our guide. He told us about how important it was to watch his every step as we ventured up because he knew the best route and all the right rocks to step on.

To my surprise, he grabbed my hand and told everyone else to link together and follow. My husband took my hand and behind us there were about twenty people following.

Footsteps of My Lord

I heard you in the morning, Lord,
Stepping softly on the leaves
Nudging dew drops from the roses
With winter's morning breeze.

And then you stepped so lightly
Into the morning light
Your warbler sang so brightly
With sweet good-byes to the night.

Your steps grew steady in the day
Their pace so strong and sure
And straight up as the noonday sun
Their path seemed so secure.
But as the night drew close
And rain began to fall,
You tap danced on my porch
For evening's curtain call.

Sometimes I hear you stepping
On the path ahead
Your footsteps leading upward bound
Saying follow where I've led.

Your footprints laid out before me
Are written with your hand
Your scriptures impressed upon my heart
Like feet upon wet sand
Are clear and true and
Lead me to
Eternal solid ground
Where beauty grows and
True love shows
Life's meaning can be found.

And though I stumble on way
My feet do falter and fall,
Because you walked down Calvary's road
I'll step along eternal paths
When I hear your call.

Iris Carignan

I watched each and every step the guide made with great intent and focus that day. I was aware that the safety and well-being of all who followed me was in my hands. None of the other followers could see exactly where the guide was stepping. After a few missteps, slips and falls into the cold water, we all arrived drenched but safely at the top of the waterfall.

Later, after arriving back home from this amazing trip, I found myself reminiscing on all we had experienced. I don't recall exactly when it hit me, but it occurred to me that our experience on the waterfall was a beautiful metaphor for the importance of a good and responsible Christian walk. Both my husband and I have had the privilege to serve in various leadership roles in church and other venues. We know how critical it is, especially as Christians, and even more as leaders to follow the Lord's footsteps and to watch our own steps in life. After all, we know that many will be watching, even some we aren't aware of. Psalm 17:5 says "Uphold my steps in your paths, that my footsteps may not slip." If we misstep in our faith walk, it could cause others to misstep and fall as well. If we venture off the path He has laid out before us, we will find ourselves in danger of falling.

Everyone has witnessed someone in a position of authority or leadership who *fell* through sin. It may have been a political leader in a high position or even the pastor of your own church. The wake of destruction that often follows behind such persons is always devastating. A whole nation may suffer because a president chooses to commit sin. Whole congregations have fallen away because their pastor sinned gravely. An entire denomination may suffer if sin is left unchecked. Likewise, if we aren't careful whom we follow and the path they are leading us on, we might end up stepping into something unpleasant.

Many people will try to smooth over the effects of poor leadership mistakes and say that their sin is their own personal matter, but sin never affects only the person who commits it. A moral trespass is especially damaging and far-reaching, even to succeeding generations. Even if you are not in a position of leadership, every person who identifies as a "Christian" (Christ follower) has a responsibility to walk in a way that honors Him. James 3:1 tells us that, "Not many of you should presume to be teachers, my brothers, because you know that we who teach will be judged more strictly." Teachers and leaders in the church need to be especially careful in their faith walk. What we do and say reflects on the whole church body and ultimately on the Lord. The only way we can do this is through the power of His Holy Spirit and by following His steps as laid out in the Bible. As it says in Psalm 119: 105, "Your word is a lamp unto my feet and a light unto my path."

Full Circle Smile

One of my favorite comediennes, Phyllis Diller, once said: *"A smile is a curve that sets everything straight."* God demonstrated this to me once, with surprising irony.

My first real job was working as a cashier or "checker" as we called it then. It was a small market and hard work, but it paid well. Even my youthful eighteen-year-old legs had begun showing signs of varicose veins from long hours of standing on a concrete floor. The constant bending over to lift groceries from the customer's basket to the counter was beginning to wear on my young back as well. Yet, despite all the many reasons for calling it "work," I enjoyed my job and greeted every customer with a cheerful smile. To me it was an opportunity to meet and greet many new friends and indeed that is how I met the man I married. That of course, is a whole other story. Naturally, not everyone who came through my checkout line was pleasant and some were downright difficult. However, I continued my best efforts to "not grow weary while doing good."

When I became engaged to that extra special customer, my natural carbonated personality seemed to be magnified beyond containment. Apparently some of my customers noticed as I called out prices and punched the old register keys with a double dose of cheer. However, reality's harsh hand caught me off duty one day and slapped the smile right off my face. It was my day off and I was shopping for my wedding-night negligee. Finding a pretty nightgown that would make my boyish figure look sexy was a task that took its toll on my spirits. I had decided that this was the last boutique I would try, when a familiar woman entered the same shop. Although by now I knew many customers by name, she was only vaguely familiar. In recognition of me as "her checker", she spoke first. Surprised to see that I wasn't my usual cheerful self, she began telling me how I had so often helped her get through a difficult day. "Sometimes," she said, "I would think of a reason to go grocery shopping just so I could see your smiling face."

My figure didn't miraculously change at that moment, but I'm sure the countenance on my face returned to its former glow. The smile I had given her now reflected back on me brighter than any mirror might show. My own smile had come back full circle to me. We never know how our attitude may affect someone else, but I try to remember to "not grow weary while doing good, for in due season we shall reap if we do not lose heart" (Galatians 6:7–10).

Chapter 11

Unexpected Holiday Perspectives

An Awesome Perspective

As our plane approached LAX on the evening of our return from a vacation, suddenly several people began making o-o-o-h sounds. I glanced out my window and saw a most amazing and surprising sight—fireworks exploding everywhere for miles. It was an awesome and most interesting perspective of our nation's birthday celebration for the 4th of July. Of course, I have seen many fireworks displays over the years, but never from a heavenly perspective.

I couldn't help but wonder at that point what God thinks and feels as He looks down from His throne, not only at the colorful splashes of glittering fireworks in California but all across our nation. Does it make him joyous to see us celebrating our blessings and heritage or does He weep over the vain partying of a nation that has strayed far from the faith it was founded on? Still, it was an awesome and unusual sight for us that night and we were happy to celebrate in a new way.

After sharing this experience with some friends, they shared an experience they'd had while on vacation in Belgium. It wasn't for the 4th of July, of course, but for another important commemoration. This was a grand celebration of the end of WWII. Our friends told of how they were in a restaurant with a large picture window nearby that looked out over a valley. Suddenly they began to see hundreds of fireworks shooting off into the sky. They learned that at midnight, the colorful display would end and the whole city would be totally dark in silent reverence of all who had lost their lives during that horrible war. Now *that* sounded like a well-balanced and meaningful commemoration.

Freedom's Never Free

There is a land
Of which I'm certain
Is a land of the brave and free.

It was built by our great fathers.
Built for you and built for me.
It wasn't born without a trial,
Nor did it happen easily.

The men who died
To bring us freedom,
Gave their lives for you and me.

So when you stand and see old glory,
Or when you sit by the shining sea,

Just think of all that came before it,
And that freedom 's never free.

To look ahead to our great future,
This land I love
Must see the past.

For it was there
Our nation's history,
The great foundation's built to last.
It is a land of strength and power,
With its' roots of faith and peace.
It is a land of great resources,
A land of opportunity.

So when you stand and see Old Glory,
Or when you sit by the shining sea,
Just think of all that went before it,
And that freedom's never free.
    Music and lyrics by Iris Carignan, July 4, 2014

We all like to celebrate and some of us look for the smallest reason to throw a party. I wonder, though, how much of what we do for holiday celebrations like Memorial Day, 4th of July, Labor Day, Thanksgiving, Christmas and Easter etc., actually expresses or produces appreciation and reverence for their true meanings.

The Israelites were instructed by God to set markers of stone in certain places to help them remember God's leading, blessing and protection. Sometimes God told them to build altars for sacrifice as commemoration. A friend of mine who endured terrible abuse from her own mother all her life, recently purchased a stone with words on it to help her remember God's love and path for her life.

As tender creations, I believe all of humanity craves joyous reflecting on even the most horrendous events that have affected their lives. It gives them a sense of hope in the midst of sad remembrances. It sets a marker for a new and better path for the future. Psalm 121:1–2 says: "I will lift up my eyes to the hills, from whence comes my help? My help comes from the Lord, who made heaven and earth."

So, in light of the amazing heavenly perspective experienced that year, I set my heart towards a deeper appreciation of its' meaning. The following 4th of July, I felt my heart swell with emotion as I watched the fireworks give tribute and heard an inspiring musical celebration. This time the impression on my spirit brought forth a new song entitled "Freedom's Never Free" (page 170 - 171).

The Winning Ticket

The ladies' Holiday Tea was coming up again at my church, this time scheduled prior to Thanksgiving. Tickets tend to sellout quickly for this big event, so I purchased mine early and decided to get an extra one too. My intention was to invite someone who needed to grow spiritually, maybe even come to the Lord through the inspiration of the speaker. Now came the challenge of seeking God's lead on whom I should invite. After all, He knows their heart better than I. A long-time acquaintance came to mind who had recently displayed some dark influences in her heart, but her non-response to my phone call sent a clear message early on.

Other names sorted through my mind as potential invitees. One in particular popped-up several times and each time I quickly resisted it. *"Not her Lord, she is nice and has a sweet heart, but..."* My mind reasoned away this friend who brings with her a woe-is-me spirit coupled with anxious worrying. *"Who else, Lord?"* I prayed.

An acquaintance came to mind and Larry made another plausible suggestion too. The two new potential winners auditioned in my mind like skipping fairies in a forest of gnarly tree stumps that kept tripping them up. No luck there either as neither one could come. With the Tea just one day away, it appeared that my impulsive generosity on a $35 extra ticket would be for naught. Still, that name popped up again.

With just one day left, I finally relented to God's prodding and asked my "worry wart" friend if she would like to come. Her reply: "I don't know. I kinda have plans and I might catch the flu or something with all those people."

"Call me early tomorrow morning to let me know, okay?" I said, not letting her get off so easily. Friday morning came and with it the phone call from my timid friend. Her answer had moved a little closer to the "yes" zone, but her typical excuses got me wound up. With as much patience and love as I could muster, along with a quick zip line prayer, I proceeded to counsel my friend with some helps.

One hard but necessary point needed to be said, that her constant worrying and negativity was a symptom of not trusting in God. "I never thought about that," she responded.

I continued with several comments and suggestions of spiritual exercises that could strengthen her efforts, but affirming God's love as greater than any parent or husband could give her. That point seemed to encourage her spirit the most. After about thirty minutes of phone counsel, I begged off for an appointment that loomed over my head. I said she needed to pray over her decision and call me no later than noon with her answer, so I could return the unused ticket to the church if she wasn't going.

The phone rang right on time—"I decided to go to the Holiday Tea."

"That's great!" I gleefully shouted.

The event began beautifully with good fellowship around a pretty table and a boutique where I was able to sell a few of my Viadorne handbags. But, how would it go with the speaker and entertainment? My friend was an excellent musician. Would the quality of the performance please her? Would the speaker talk too much about family matters that my single friend couldn't relate to? We took our seats in the auditorium and were immediately impressed with the musical mother/daughter duet on stage. The speaker walked in and I recognized her immediately as a very lovely woman who had stopped by my boutique booth and encouraged my heart. My own anxious thoughts disappeared.

With a slow, easy-going style, the speaker opened our hearts and ears to the topic of the evening—*Preparing Our Hearts for the Holidays.* Poking fun at her own shortcomings and "perfectionist" holiday aspirations, she further endeared herself to the audience. Then, with graceful cadence, she began unwrapping her own tender heart and difficult childhood with uncanny familiarity.

Her story seemed so similar to my friend's; you would think it was a planned scheme. Furthermore, she continued to give point-by-point instructions that struck home with my friend and coincided perfectly with the counseling I'd given her that very same morning. Turning to my companion with shrugged shoulders and hushed excitement, I insisted that I had no idea the message would be about the same thing.

"Really?" She asked.

My friend grabbed a torn piece of scrap paper from her purse and began taking notes. The speaker went on expounding in many inspirational ways and reaffirming so much of what I'd tried to express earlier. Verse after verse further reinforced the message of God's love for my friend.

Noticing tears, I offered her the clean handkerchief given me as a favor at last year's Holiday Tea. The message received that night sank deep into my friend's heart, and was one we both knew held lasting meaning for more than just the holidays. Could it be that my Lord had orchestrated the whole evening just for my friend? He surely directed my actions toward the name that kept "popping-up" in contrast to the rejecting friends. He played out His hand for the one who needed the "winning ticket" and directions toward a joyous life. He even gave her a scripture of encouragement for those first steps: Jeremiah 29:11 "For I know the plans I have for you, plans to prosper you not to harm you, says the Lord." It happened to be the same verse I had quoted to her earlier that day.

Unexpected Fruit

"Just get over it!" my son said as the remaining shards of glass were being swept up. One of my prettiest wine goblets had smashed down on the table as he and my husband pulled at the table to add another leaf. "It's just a glass and more importantly, your guests will be much more comfortable now that we've added the other table leaf." He went on with a never mind that I'd warned them to remove the glasses before adding it. It was Thanksgiving and for some unknown reason, the goblins of mischief that had plagued us all month seemed to still be lurking in our midst.

"But, you don't understand," I protested. "I set this table three days ago and aside from having all the family together, setting a pretty table is very important to me."

Of course, I knew my son was right about what was truly important that day, but not only had I told them to take off the glasses as a precaution, this minor foible seemed perfectly timed by the same Grinch who had stalked us for more than a month. The shattering sound of the breaking glass might just as well have been a clanging bell signaling the end of round six and the start of another in this boxing match of disappointments and changes to our holiday celebration. You see, this wasn't just another Thanksgiving, this year we were also celebrating our 45th wedding anniversary, yet hard as we tried, everything we planned had been changed several times.

Glancing at the formal dining room table, I sighed at the now imperfect balance to my arrangement. Just days ago, the table looked bountifully splendid, decked with the heirloom brass and crystal scales that had formerly graced the tables of my mother and grandmother. Surrounding the scales was a colorful wreath of leaves that seemed to symbolize our family circle. Spilling over one of the crystal holding trays of the scale, I'd placed luscious looking, yet fake, grapes weighing the scales heavier against a few nuts, a small pear and a gourd in the other tray. Balancing out my table composition and weakly guarding the tableware were the "wood" carved pilgrim figures at each end. Now as I surveyed the adjusted table, my heart sank at the vision before me—everything was off-center from the chandelier above it.

On top of that, I needed to add another charger plate that would not match the others already set out. We were expecting nineteen people for this year's celebration and I'd worked hard to get all three tables beautifully set, but it had become obvious that we needed to move one person from the informal table to the formal dining room to make it comfortable. Clearly my perfectionist and artistic notions were being played like a fiddle by the one who knows how best to turn our talents into flaws— the Prince of schemes and the Thief of the ages. So, I let it go. After all, maybe the arrangement represented our family's off-centeredness and human flaws most appropriately.

Beginning more than four months ago with some initial plans, Larry and I had adjusted our sights as to how this year would bring our family together. We had hoped to use all of our timeshare points at a new section of our main resort in Escondido, where we could all gather and play . When it became obvious that plan A wasn't going to work, we had gone to plan B. Resolved to simplify things for our grown children, we decided to have a Thanksgiving–Anniversary celebration at a restaurant with the family. Then the two of us would go to a timeshare resort in Cabo San Lucas, Mexico for a romantic getaway. Our children seemed content with the plan and we were thrilled to learn that our son and his family, who lived in Northern California, would be coming down to join us too.

August blew into September, but not before a huge storm also blew into Mexico. A powerful hurricane struck the very area where we had planned to stay. News reports told of several resorts being heavily damaged and folks being stranded without shelter, food or a flight home. I wondered if our resort was also part of the collateral damage. We waited to hear news from our timeshare company as September rolled into October and November peeked into view. "Surely they would have contacted us if it had been badly damaged," I comforted myself, but nagging worries pushed me into calling to check.

"I'm calling to make sure everything is still good with our reservation in Cabo," I told the timeshare rep.

"Oh no, it's been cancelled" she chirped as if giving me happy news.

"What?"

"Yes, we've put all your points back into your account."

"Why didn't you tell us?" I nearly shouted at her. "We have airfare already booked and were supposed to be leaving in less than a month."

The rep rambled on, cheerfully unconcerned at our now sudden and urgent predicament. "Don't worry" she went on, "the resort will be up and open again by April and you can go then."

"But our anniversary is in November!" I emphasized with restrained anger.

"Oh" was all she could muster at that point.

Lord, what should we do now?

So, plan C was quickly hustled in and a new romantic destination opened to us. Although it was too late to use our timeshare points, we were able to book a last minute deal on a cruise to the Caribbean. We kept the basic family plan in place and a reservation at a nice restaurant was made. The restaurant manager assured me of the traditional Thanksgiving dinner menu, a private room with fireplace and a time of 2 p.m.

Another week flew by, placing the event just two weeks away when the restaurant called. "We see you have a 2 p.m. reservation and we want you to know that the Thanksgiving menu will not be served until 5 p.m."

"That won't work," I protested, "some of our family have a long drive home and little children to attend. But go ahead and give us the 5 p.m. time slot and we will try to work it out."

"Oh, we can't do that; we have another large party at 5:30," she informed me.

"Then what *can* you give us?"

"The earliest we can do is 7:45 p.m."

"Forget it!" I retorted, and hung up.

Two days later, I reserved not one, but two restaurants just to be safe. Both of the new places reserved were very nice, even nicer than the one canceled, but neither could give us a private room. Would it work well for the combined celebration, I wondered. Pushing the nagging thought to the back of my mind, I trudged on with other plans.

With about a week and a half left before the holiday on a Monday evening, we got a call from our eldest. Larry took the call and I could tell by his concerned expression that something else was brewing.

"What was that all about?" I asked hesitantly.

Larry struggled to explain as delicately as possible that our kids had been talking about the upcoming event. They were "concerned" that having it at a restaurant wouldn't work so well. "You have got to be kidding! I can't believe this—another change!" Tears of disappointment and frustration now spilled out with just cause. *What is going on, Lord?* I pleaded. *Are you trying to tell me something?* Maybe this is a new fruit of the Spirit— *flexibility.* It certainly runs a close in-kind to patience. Perhaps it's a variety—you know, like Fuji apples verses Gala apples. Or maybe it's like a shriveled plum, now called a prune. Whatever this whole ever-changing lesson had been about, my spirits and emotions had experienced more changes than a chameleon walking on a multicolored autumn leaf.

After calming from the initial shock, my creative mind went to work figuring out a new plan that suited my expectations. We would decorate the patio with pretty white lights and maybe a few stars hanging down, order a cake and have the second half of the family gathering as an early evening anniversary celebration. My revised vision excited me as I thought about the view from our backyard, which is more stunning than any restaurant in town anyway. Who knows, maybe we could even do a little romantic dancing out there too. Okay, this is finally shaping up to be what I was hoping for. I canceled both restaurant reservations and opted to order catered food from a restaurant. The kids promised to help serve and clean up; *that remained to be seen.*

Larry got busy decorating; I found just the right stars to hang from our patio cover, and then ordered a cake. An invitation was sent to all the family and a note on it informed them that we planned to dress in our *best* for the occasion. I wanted this to feel special in every way for all.

So here it was—the big day. The formal table was finally ready and all were gathered in a circle to pray and give thanks to the

Lord. The moment of connection with family united in prayer seemed to hang on longer than time usually permits. The meal was scrumptious and our eldest pitched in, faithfully helping to serve and clean up. The kids came in their Sunday best (for some that meant their "best" blue jeans, but I held my tongue). My legs and feet ached as I worked to serve in high heels and a new dress. The evening flowed on into the night with our anniversary celebration sparkling as brightly as the draped lights on our patio deck.

God gave us an unseasonably hot day (90 degrees) that warmed the coolness of the setting sun perfectly for outdoor activities. The cake was cut, a new poem for my Honey was recited, and Larry and I danced to one of our favorite songs by Neil Diamond— "Sweet Caroline." I knew the song well, but didn't realize until that moment how appropriate my new poem was. The lyrics crooned on about hands holding hands and touching. The poem I'd written especially for Larry was entitled *His Touch* and was my expression of how special my husband's hands and touch were to me—they are the hands of a carpenter, yet gentle and caring like the hands that created them.

With tired feet and bodies, we finally rested awhile as we opened all the unexpected gifts lavished on us that evening. More unexpected though, were the gifts that poured out most generously from our Lord that evening—the gifts of the Holy Spirit. He had made sure our celebration shone brightly with love, joy, peace, patience, kindness, goodness, faithfulness, gentleness, self-control and even a new fruit—*flexibility.*

"But the fruit of the Spirit is love, joy, peace, patience, kindness, goodness, faithfulness, gentleness and self-control. Against such things there is no law" (Galatians 5:22–23 NIV).

The Fruit (No. 3 in the Trilogy)

The fruit of the Spirit
Is evidence to see
Of God who is living inside you and me,
But left in the basket only for display
Twill lose its sweetness
Rot and wither away.

It must be ingested by others nearby
To plant seeds in their hearts
And grow more fruit by and by.

The fruit of His Spirit
Love, joy and some peace
Just a few are needed most days, at least.
But sometimes a fruit salad
Of all He can give
Make for a better
Way for each of us to live.

We can't make this sweet fruit on our own
No straining and effort will
Make spiritual fruit be grown.
No, it only sprouts from the seed
Of His love
Planted in our hearts
From His Spirit above.

By Iris Carignan 1/2/2015

Distracted Focus and Missed Blessing

How many times have we all found ourselves driving along a road or highway, daydreaming, and in an instant lose sight of where we are or where we are going? We've all missed a sign or turn and took an unplanned route as a result of our inattention. Our own personal distractions, foggy spiritual focus, as well as the storms of life can take us off course or cause us to miss out on blessings waiting along the way.

It was just such a day about thirty years ago, when my languid response to an opportunity resulted in a missed blessing and years of regret. I was at a choir rehearsal that evening and the director realized that we needed more copies of the music we were learning. Our pianist, the pastor's wife, and I, volunteered to go down to the church office to get the needed copies.

The sun was close to setting and a light rain had begun to fall as we entered the office that evening. Finished with our business and having turned off the light, we stepped out into the garden path. Startling our exit, several strangers approached us. All of them were dressed in biblical-style attire. One of them came closer and introduced himself as a fellow believer and "traveler". He then asked if the church might have a room where they could rest for the night and be sheltered from the rain. I started to respond positively but was quickly cut short by my companion. "We don't have the authority for that," she responded. Of course, being the pastor's wife, she did indeed have the authority, but was obviously wary of allowing strangers onto church property.

"It doesn't take authority," the young man said "It just takes heart!" The strangers walked away briskly and we stared at each other with pricked consciousness.

"Maybe we could let them sleep in the early childhood room where there's a bathroom," she revised.

"Sure," I said and immediately we set out to find them and give them hospitable good news. They couldn't have been out of our sight for more than a few seconds, yet as we rounded the other side of the building in their direction, they were nowhere to be seen. They had simply vanished. There were no other structures nearby to hide the conspicuously dressed group, and no crowds of people to blend in with, yet we could not see them anywhere.

Looking at each other in wonder and dismay, words failed and expressions revealed our obvious regret and curiosity of the blessing we both missed that night. We had forgotten to entertain strangers and likely missed out on "entertaining angels." Perhaps there is no correlation to this event, but it was only a few years later that the church closed its doors.

Can you imagine the regret the innkeepers had for turning away Mary and Joseph that serendipitous night? After learning later of the special birth they missed, it must have pierced their hearts with remorse. Some no doubt never put it together, or made excuses for their harshness and unsympathetic refusal of a room. We can only surmise that many may have realized their mistake and lived with regret for the blessing missed. Who knows, but perhaps some of the inns may have even gone out of business consequently. Hebrews 13:2 shines a light on the importance of attentiveness and brotherly love while on life's highway: "Let brotherly love continue. Do not forget to entertain strangers, for by so doing some have unwittingly entertained angels."

A Beautiful Christmas Sight

Perhaps it was the brush of an angel that woke me that morning, or maybe it was just my husband's restlessness. Whatever the case, something woke me from my deep slumber with a frightful start.

In my dreamy sleep, I thought I heard the sound of someone walking through the house. It wasn't a loud crashing noise, but a soft shuffling, like feet across the carpet. Despite the subtle sound, I awoke with heart-thumping concern. My heavy eyelids resisted opening and my first thought was that we might have a prowler, considering it was Christmas and there were presents lying under our tree. I prayed a silent prayer of protection. Attempting to comfort myself with reason, I thought about other possibilities for the shuffling sound. Perhaps it was one of the children wandering the halls and feeling ill. Maybe curiosity had gotten the best of one of the kids and they were trying to get a peek at their gifts.

Forcing my eyes to open in spite of the sleepy glue that sealed them shut, I tried to listen more intently, but heard nothing. I considered just going back to sleep, but, I needed to go to the bathroom, so I got up. With some trepidation, I glanced down our long hallway as I cautiously made my way to the bathroom. On my return trip I took one more look, but there still was no sign of anyone. Just to be sure, I decided to look out our bedroom window for any evidence of an intruder.

To my amazement and awe, there it was—the most beautiful star I'd ever seen. Surely, it was the reason I'd been wakened. I blinked my sleepy eyes and waited to be certain it wasn't some sort of aircraft. It almost seemed to hover and was clearly brighter and bigger than all the other stars in the sky. I've seen the morning star, called Sirius, but this was much larger and more brilliant by far. Then, I remembered hearing a report on television a few days earlier about a special constellation in the sky that was going to be visible. They said something about it possibly being the same sight that brought those famous, wise astronomers, or Magi, as the Bible tells, to Christ's birth 2000 years ago.

Excitement rose inside and I wanted to wake everyone in the house, so they could see it too. Glancing at the clock, I noted the time was a very early 4 a.m., and considered the consequences of waking four grumpy people. Motherly wisdom vetoed this idea. With joyful exuberance flooding my heart, I hoped my husband's earlier restlessness meant he was at least half awake.

"Are you awake?" I whispered gently as I slipped back into bed.

"No," he said.

"I just saw the most beautiful star ever!"

"What were you doing outside at this hour?" He mumbled in a gravelly voice that had a sleep-deprived edge to it.

"I wasn't outside. I just looked out the bedroom window. It might be the same star the wise men saw at Christ's birth."

His reply came with surprising alertness and revelation as he asked if the star was in the eastern part of the sky.

"Yes! Yes! It was in the eastern sky," I nearly squealed back.

"I'll see it when I get up later," he said, rolling over.

Saying a prayer of thanksgiving for the special Christmas gift He had given me that early morning, I fell blissfully back to sleep.

Whether it was the nudge of an angel or the Holy Spirit that woke me on that morning thirty years ago, this experience continues to shine in my heart today. It is one more amazing sign of the Lord's meticulous and stellar details related to the birth of the Messiah. The Magi, or wise men, were not only excellent astronomers, they knew about the prophecies told hundreds of years earlier in the Old Testament. They not only observed the sign, but acted on it in great faith by traveling hundreds of miles to witness this miracle for themselves and to worship the newborn king it foretold.

"I see him, but not now; I behold him, but not near. A star will come out of Jacob; a scepter will rise out of Israel" (Numbers 24:17). In the gospel of Matthew, we see the fulfillment of this prophecy as well as other prophecies regarding the Messiah. Matthew 2:2 (NIV) says: "After Jesus was born in Bethlehem in Judea, during the time of King Herod, Magi from the east came to Jerusalem and asked "Where is the one who has been born king of the Jews? We saw his star in the east and have come to worship him."

But For the Joy

While on my usual morning walk, something caught my eye. It was a tiny palm tree growing, amazingly, through the black asphalt of our street. The little seedling was barely three inches high. As impressive as its fortitude was, the shadow it cast was larger and more interesting because of its shape—a cross. The irony struck immediately with clear prophetic meaning. This pint sized plant seemed to be forecasting a reminder and fate from the past. It stood proudly proclaiming the former glory of its use on a day of celebration, the triumphal entry of the King and Messiah into Jerusalem. Its baby leaves stretched towards the sunlight like the loving arms of our Lord and their shadow predicting the coming crucifixion. It seemed that it was doing its best to compensate (in a small way) for the turnabout. What had begun as a joyous celebration and laying of palm branches as a carpet for the coming King, had so quickly turned to condemnation, cursing and hanging on a tree.

This startling sight occurred just days before Christmas, and as I pondered the timing of this prophetic picture, my spirit reveled in its hopeful, all-inclusive meaning. The newborn purity of this infant tree was to me another baby, a baby in a manger. It too had an inhospitable environment for birthing. Seeing the enduring strength of this baby plant that had triumphed over the stubborn hardness of asphalt spoke to my soul. Its victory over struggle beautifully modeled some of the pain, suffering and resistance Jesus experienced, even prior to the cross.

Jesus warned his friends about His coming death when He said: "I tell you the truth, unless a kernel of wheat falls to the ground and dies, it remains only a single seed. But if it dies, it produces many seeds" (John 12:24 NIV). He knew His time was drawing near and soon He would face the ultimate enemy—death. Hundreds of years before Jesus the Christ came to earth, another prophet foretold of the Messiah in a similar way. Isaiah 53 most notably prophesied the Messiah as one who "grew up before him like a tender shoot, and like a root out of dry ground...He was despised and rejected by men, a man of sorrows, and familiar with suffering....Surely he took up our infirmities and carried our sorrows, yet we considered him stricken by God, smitten by him, and afflicted...But he was pierced for our transgressions, he was crushed for our iniquities; the punishment that brought us peace was upon him, and by his wounds we are healed."

Take a few minutes to read all of Isaiah's words of great prophecy alongside the Calvary story and be prepared for God's amazing foreshadowing of redemption and grace. With each approaching day, let your eyes be focused and your ears be tuned to receive any sign that He has prepared for you as reminder of His love and sacrifice.

If you're going through a season of struggle, look to the victory that brings us hope and to the victor who brought it—Jesus.

Chapter 12

Keeping the Goal in Sight

Finding Our Stride

While watching the movie "Secretariat," I was at once enthralled with the nobility of racehorses. Seeing this magnificent creature of God display it's amazing strength, power and forceful endurance was breathtaking. The thundering gallop and connection with the ground to catapult it forward gracefully was in itself inspiring. This rhythmic sound seemed to reach into my own soul and draw forth a measure of God's essence.

The book of Job reveals God's creative intent was fulfilled in this animal. He questions Job's comprehension of its intricate characteristics. "Do you give the horse his strength or clothe his neck with a flowing mane? Do you make him leap like a locust, striking terror with his proud snorting? He paws fiercely, rejoicing in his strength and charges into the fray" (Job 39:19–22).

The movie kept my attention as I watched Secretariat take his imposing body headlong towards the finish line, with muscular legs that seemed disproportionately small yet all too agile.

About the time I began to feel satiated with this glorious creature, a new perspective grabbed my attention. Atop this majestic high station rode its jockey. With typical lightweight, diminutive size, he made for the perfect pairing for success. I considered how the rider must feel as he becomes one with the horse, experiencing its power, strength. and exhilarating force flow through his spirit. I imagine that for the rider, each thrilling yet transitory moment is fulfilling God's purpose for his life. No doubt, men of small stature struggle in their comparative walks alongside the common male height. Yet, during these brief times of skillful exuberance, they find their stride in life with tall satisfaction. What a beautiful metaphor for all believers, equestrian or not, as we ride through life. It is a clear illustration of the importance of "laying aside every weight, and the sin which so easily ensnares us" (Hebrews 12:1b).

As swiftly as the race rounds another bend, my thoughts turn to the beauty of the metaphor racing by. We are, after all, miniscule in stature next to our great and mighty God. Truly, we are only powerful when we learn to let our Lord's strength charge through our spirit. It is by His strength that we can do all things, not by our own. When we become one with the Lord in purpose and goal, we harness His power, like the jockey whose horse takes him to the finish line. Whether we are at the pinnacle of a life changing moment or working our way through everyday stuff, only through His might and strength will we run the race He has set before us.

God continues his challenge to Job in chapter 39:22–25, describing the horse and its strength. "He laughs at fear, afraid of nothing and doesn't shy away from the sword. In frenzied excitement he eats up the ground and he cannot stand still when the trumpet sounds." I pray that my Lord will make me feel that way about each and every day that He gives me.

Running the Race in Stride

Dedicated to Brandon Carignan

Oh that we should ride on the strength of the Lord
Each and every day of our race.
Oh, that we would let His swift and powerful legs
Continue to set the pace.

Oh, that each day's trumpet would
Open the gate and start us with great vigor,
And harnessed to Him 't would carry our spirits
With all of His might and rigor.

Imagine the power intertwined as one
From the start of the gate 'til setting of sun.

Take off the weight of all that deters,
Let us not stumble on things that hinder
From the goal set before us our eyes fixed ahead,
We'll make it someday if we follow where led.

Sometimes the horse,
Sometimes the rider,
Sometimes the dirt on the ground.
Whatever my lot, whatever my station,
I pray that my heart will be found
Eager to run
Eager to follow

The pull of His reins on my life.
And full of His strength
Not in the fodder,
I'll run in the grace of each strife.

Carried to the finish and
Running for roses,
The race can never be won,
Without perseverance,
Without some endurance,
Without His might and His Son.

Iris Carignan, 5/ 17/15

Alohas

Anyone who speaks the most basic Hawaiian knows that the word *aloha* can mean either hello or good-bye. I know that many readers like to go straight to the end to see how the story comes out. So, whether you are just starting this journey with me or you are finishing it, I pray the message of this collection will be an "aloha" to you. May its tidings of purpose, protection, and guidance be planted in the soil of your heart and become a welcome to God's leading for each new day. May it also be farewell to the doubts that lie in wait along the path of each journey and threaten to steal your joy and hope.

It is my prayer that it has given you fresh eyes and encouraged you to look expectantly for God in all circumstances of life. If a story or scripture remains in your heart and sharpens your spiritual vision, or evokes devotion to our Lord, may all praise and glory be given to God's Holy Spirit for His leading in this work. If it has awakened the awareness of God's hand in your life, it has become bread upon the waters of your heart and will accomplish what He purposes.

There is another word that also has the dual meaning of hello and farewell and that word is Shalom. More than just a greeting or send-off, the essence of Shalom is a prayer wrapped in peace to all who receive it. Wherever God has taken you in your journey of faith thus far, and at whatever point in time this has found you, may the gleanings you have gained be greetings of hello to each new experience and a path to peace wherever you go.

So, until we meet again on another *sightseeing* journey, *aloha* and *shalom* to every traveler God brings my way.

Unending Love

"My days are like the evening shadow; I wither away like grass. Let this be written for a future generation, that a people not yet created may praise the Lord" (Psalm 102:11 & 18 NIV).

Sunset Contrast

I love to watch the sunset
Fall with grace upon the night;
It reminds me of the color
Christ has brought into my life.

The contrast of the dark shapes
Up against the light,
Cutting the horizon
With a sharpness clear and bright.

Like me next to my Savior
A purpose does it show,
Of the glory of the Father
Holy Spirit and Son to know.

Keep my direction bound to the Light
And source of all beauty
With strength on through the night.
Turn my light on Lord,
Let it shine and brightly show
As the moon reflects the sun
Let me also brightly glow.

By Iris Carignan

Psalm 51:10–11 (NKJ)

"Create in me a clean heart, O God,
And renew a steadfast spirit within me.
Do not cast me away from Your presence,
And do not take Your Holy Spirit from me.

Restore to me the joy of Your salvation,
And uphold me with Your generous Spirit.
Then I will teach transgressors Your ways,
And sinners shall be converted to You"

Acknowledgments

The collection in this book would not have happened without the many people whom God has placed in my path along its journey. Joni Eareckson Tada is one such person who has been a treasured friend and encourager in this process. Her wisdom, talent and help along the way have been a blessing far too great for words. I would also like to thank my editors and friends Margery Walshaw and Joanna Mastopietro, who have continued to help in so many ways through this process. Their amazing expertise have been invaluable in so many ways. A big thank you also goes to author Joel Kilpatrick for his generous encouragement in the early stages of the book. Having his skill and talent for an assessment was a tremendous confirmation to me as a writer.

To my family, especially my husband Larry, who has stood by me and often sacrificed precious together-time during the process, I give my loving devotion and thanks. I am also very grateful for my children who encouraged me and in particular, my son Jason, who has helped on technical issues as well as marketing and publishing advice.

I am also indebted to the many friends and family who have allowed me to tell their own personal stories. Their willingness to bare their souls for the benefit and spiritual edification of the reader is a gift my Lord will surely use to bear spiritual fruit.

To all of the wonderful staff at WestBow Press and especially my team, who have been so helpful in the production, sales, and marketing of "FRESH EYES, Seeing God in the Unexpected," I am very grateful. The opportunity and expertise they offer to novice authors fills a great chasm in the publishing world.

My heart also swells gratefully for my pastor and shepherd, Shawn Thornton and to Pastor Larry De Witt, who continue to bring God's words of truth to me, and so many others, in very real and edifying ways.

Above all, I thank my God who gave me all of these stories, insights, and poetry. It is through His Son and the leading of His Holy Spirit that any and all accounts included in this episodic collection were placed here. I pray they will be to His glory and honor.